D1036064

The Late Show

Also by David Trinidad

Pavane (1981)
Monday, Monday (1985)
Living Doll (1986)
November (1987)
Three Stories (1988)
A Taste of Honey (with Bob Flanagan, 1990)
Hand Over Heart: Poems 1981-1988 (1991)
Answer Song (1994)
Essay with Movable Parts (1998)
Chain Chain Chain (with Jeffery Conway and Lynn Crosbie, 2000)
Plasticville (2000)
Phoebe 2002: An Essay in Verse (with Jeffery Conway and Lynn Crosbie, 2003)
Tiny Moon Notebook (2007)

Editor

Powerless: Selected Poems 1973-1990 by Tim Dlugos (1996)
Holding Our Own: The Selected Poems of Ann Stanford
   (with Maxine Scates, 2001)
Saints of Hysteria: A Half-Century of Collaborative American Poetry
   (with Denise Duhamel and Maureen Seaton, 2007)

The Late Show

DAVID TRINIDAD

POEMS

Turtle Point Press
New York
2007

LCCN: 2006906040
ISBN: 978-1-933527-09-3

Cover and text design by Charles Rue Woods

Turtle Point Press
233 Broadway, Room 946
New York, NY 10279

Printed in the United States of America

In memory of my mother

Acknowledgments

I am grateful to the editors of the following publications in which these poems originally appeared:

Absomaly: "Gloss of the Past"
American Letters & Commentary: "Written with a Pencil Found in Lorine
    Niedecker's Front Yard"
American Poet: "Ode to Thelma Ritter"
The American Poetry Review: "A Poet's Death"
Black Clock: "James Schuyler" and "To Tim Dlugos"
Bloom: "After Neruda"
The Canary: "Hack, Hack, Sweet Has-Been"
Columbia Poetry Review: "Classic Layer Cakes"
Combo: "Candy Necklace" and "Queen Bee"
Fourteen Hills: "The Late Show"
Gargoyle: "Penelope"
The Hat: "From the Life of Joe Brainard"
Jacket: "Doll Memorial Service"
The James White Review: "For Joe Brainard"
LIT: "All This, and Heaven Too"
The Poetry Project Newsletter: "Kid Stuff by Oscar Wilde"
Shiny: "Nature Poem"
The Solitary Plover: "Crack of old ice"
The Spoon River Poetry Review: "A Regret"
Washington Square: "To Arielle and the Moon" and "Who's There?"
Wicked Alice: "After E.D. (#873)" and "Sonnet"
The World: "Slicker" and "Watching the Late Movie with My Mother"

Portions of "A Poem Under the Influence" appeared in *Bloom, Bombay Gin, Coconut, Columbia Poetry Review, Combo, Three Candles,* and in a chapbook published by A Rest Press in 2005.

A letterpress broadside of "To Arielle and the Moon," designed by Amanda Stevenson, was printed for a reading at the Center for Book Arts in New York City on December 8, 2006.

Special thanks to Columbia College Chicago for a faculty development grant, and to the friends who read and commented on these poems as they were written: Jeanne Marie Beaumont, Rebecca Burrier, Jeffery Conway, Elaine Equi, Chris Green, Arielle Greenberg, Tony Trigilio, and Susan Wheeler.

Contents

The Late Show

The Late Show

[circa 1970]

Natalie Wood, in the middle
of reciting a Wordsworth poem,
bursts into tears and runs out
of the classroom. Carroll Baker
gasps in an oxygen tent, her
platinum Harlow hair damp
and flat. Kim Stanley throws
a champagne glass at her mother's
taxi, screaming "There is no god!
There is no god!" In a chiffon
cocktail dress and ankle-straps,
Joan Crawford staggers down
the beach, convinced her lover,
Jeff Chandler, is out to murder
her. Lana Turner learns that
she and her daughter, Sandra
Dee, are in love with the same
man. Jilted and demented, Suzy
Parker crouches in an alleyway
in a soiled trench coat, sifting
through Louis Jourdan's trash.
To avoid forging the signature
of her twin sister, whom she's killed,
Bette Davis grabs the red-hot end
of a fire iron with her writing hand.
Doris Day, in a black lace peignoir,
sobs into the telephone: "Who are
you? Why are you doing this to me?"
Julie Harris hears Hill House
beckoning, beckoning. Geraldine
Page begs Paul Newman for a fix.
Simone Signoret wipes her finger-
prints off the glass as James Caan
collapses, dead at her feet. Lee
Remick pours herself another

drink. Trembling, Ingrid Berg-
man watches the gaslights dim.
Shirley MacLaine breaks down,
admits her attraction to Audrey
Hepburn. Barbara Stanwyck tries
to keep Capucine. Elizabeth Taylor
scrawls, with lipstick, "No Sale"
across a mirror. Deborah Kerr
smolders. Shelley Winters shrieks.
Kim Novak screams and backs out
of the bell tower, into thin air.

Kid Stuff by Oscar Wilde

The Etch A Sketch is laced with fitful red,
The circling Spirographs and Hula Hoops flee,
The Water Wiggle is rising from the sea,
Like a white Barbie Doll from her bed.

And jagged brazen Balsa Planes fall
Athwart the Magic Slate of the night,
And a long Slinky of yellow light
Breaks silently on Thingmaker and hall,

And spreading Silly Putty across the wold,
Wakes into View-Master some fluttering bird,
And all the Mexican Jumping Beans are stirred,
And all the Coloring Books streaked with gold.

Slicker

came in a pink,
orange and white
striped metal tube,
with a black curlicue
border and a splayed
gold base. It came
in any number of
mod shades: Nippy
Beige, Chelsea Pink,
Poppycock, Hot Nec-
taringo, Pinkadilly,
Dicey Peach. There
were several tubes in
my mother's makeup
drawer in the bath-
room five out of six
of us used (my father
had his own bathroom,
as forbidden as the
walk-in closet where
his *Playboys* were
hidden under a stack
of sweaters on the top
shelf). All the girls
at school had Slicker
in their purses; I
watched them apply
The London Look
at the beginning and
end of each class. I
marveled at what else
spilled out: compact,
mascara brush, eye
shadow, wallet, troll
doll, dyed rabbit's
foot, chewing gum,

tampon, pink plastic
comb. At home I
stared at myself in
the medicine cabinet
mirror and, as my
brother pounded
on the locked bath-
room door, twisted
a tube and rubbed,
ever so slightly,
Slicker on my lips.

Gloss of the Past

Pink Dawn, Aurora Pink, Misty Pink, Fresh Pink, Natural Pink, Country Pink, Dusty Pink, Pussywillow Pink, Pink Heather, Pink Peony, Sunflower Pink, Plum Pink, Peach of a Pink, Raspberry Pink, Watermelon Pink, Pink Lemonade, Bikini Pink, Buoy Buoy Pink, Sea Shell Pink, Pebble Pink, Pink Piper, Acapulco Pink, Tahiti Beach Pink, Sunny Pink, Hot Pink, Sizzling Pink, Skinnydip Pink, Flesh Pink, Transparent Pink, Breezy Pink, Sheer Shiver Pink, Polar Bare Pink, Pink Frost, Frosty Pink, Frost Me Pink, Frosted Pink, Sugarpuff Pink, Ice Cream Pink, Lickety Pink, Pink Melba, Pink Whip, Pinkermint, Sweet Young Pink, Little Girl Pink, Fragile Pink, Fainting Pink, Helpless Pink, Tiny Timid Pink, Wink of Pink, Shadow of Pink, Tint of Pink, Shimmer of Pink, Flicker of Pink, Pink Flash, E.S. Pink, Person-to-Person Pink, City Pink, Penny Lane Pink, Pink Paisley, London Luv Pink, Pretty Pink, Pastel Pink, Pinking Sheer, Pink Piqué, Pink Silk, Plush Pink, Lush Iced Pink, Brandied Pink, Sheer Pink Champagne, Candlelight Pink, Fluffy Moth Pink, Softsilver Pink, Pinkyring, Turn Pale Pink, A Little Pink, Pinker, Pinkety Pink, Heart of Pink, Hug that Pink, Passionate Pink, Snuggle Pink, Pink-Glo!, Happy-Go-Pink, Daredevil Pink, By Jupiter Pink, Stark Raving Pink, Viva La Pink.

Candy Necklace

[from notebooks/for Joe]

"The world is full of strange arrangements."

*

Chapel of Precious Memories

*

"The girl could not control herself. The boy was homosexual. Parents drank."

*

"Personality is holy."

—Alice Notley

*

9/2/89: Jimmy on phone machine: "Well, my name is James Schuyler and I write poetry in my spare time. And, well, am I being a bore?"

*

Kaleidoscope

*

"powder room insults"

*

Michael Feingold on Colleen Dewhurst:

When she spoke, the effect was dislocating and brilliant, because her voice, though appropriately big, was unexpectedly vulnerable, marked with quavers and frogged around the edges with the rasp of a thousand cigarettes. ("It's what Eternity would sound like," a friend said after the revival of *Moon for the Misbegotten*, "if it smoked too much.")

*

Meet Miss Truly Fucked

— Taylor Mead

*

DREAM

I found the right black sweater.

1/29/89

*

LIZ FIRES COOK FOR MAKING HER FAT!

*

the thundering
dough balls of bygone days

— Connie Deanovich

*

11/3/89: Alice on phone: "Hold on, there's a stripper on *Night Court*."

*

"Four generations of criminally insane people."

*

John Updike on Lana Turner:

One of the few photographs that capture an individual beauty was taken in the harrowing aftermath of Stompanato's death. She was wearing dark glasses and a bandanna, and the stoically pursed lips tell it all: a bleached blonde who's been around, retreating into herself as flashbulbs beat on her white skin.

*

The secret
word in my
dream was

ANNETTE

*

Good Morning Slicker

*

"I used so much hair spray that I feel personally responsible for global warming."

— Dusty Springfield

*

"He's easy on the eyes."

— Jimmy Schuyler

*

Style is an absolute way of seeing things.

— Flaubert

*

"It seemed she spent the Onassis years behind a pair of sunglasses."

*

"I am on an adventure in a different sweater."

—Susie Timmons

*

The House of a Thousand Fabrics

*

"Each line should have a shimmer in it."

—Allen Ginsberg

*

Cocktail Parasols

*

Flicker Ring

*

"two legendary ladies of the silver screen"

From the Life of Joe Brainard

[1965]

Moves
to new
apart-
ment.

Inspired
by the
color
scheme

of *The
Umbrellas
of Cherbourg*,
paints

the walls
in vari-
ous pastel
shades,

but
when
result
disap-

points
him,
moves
again.

For Joe Brainard

I remember when I met Joe Brainard. My first trip to New York City. October, 1982. Tim Dlugos took me to an art opening and introduced me to Joe in the center of the room. I was so nervous I bumped into him, causing him to spill his drink.

I remember my first crush on another boy. Roy Ruth, who was a year and a half ahead of me at Superior Street Elementary School. Before he graduated, I approached him and asked him to sign my blue autograph book. He looked surprised, but signed his name.

I remember when all the girls in our classroom were invited to a "special" film in the auditorium. I couldn't understand why I wasn't invited too. None of the girls would tell me what it was about. They'd received pink invitations.

I remember when Tommy Merande, our next-door neighbor, told my brother and me that he'd walked into his parents' bedroom without knocking and seen his mother's breasts. She'd slapped him across the face—hard. Long after they'd moved away, we heard that Mrs. Merande had died of breast cancer. I instantly remembered the story Tommy had told us.

I remember during another trip to New York, at a party at Danceteria, snorting coke with Joe in a bathroom stall.

I remember the first time I came. While "fooling around" with Hal Weiland, a blond boy who lived two doors down the street. We were alone in my house, lying on the living room floor. I didn't know what was happening, but he kept rubbing my cock until. . . . It left a faint stain on our brand-new beige carpet, which I prayed my mother wouldn't notice.

I remember Hal and I "fooling around" whenever we could. Mostly just rubbing together, touching each other's cocks. One day his mother came home and discovered us in his bedroom. After that, we never "fooled around" again.

I remember playing strip poker with the other boys in the neighborhood. On summer afternoons. Each time someone lost all of his clothes, he had to do whatever the others wanted. Like bending over and separating his cheeks (or something equally humiliating). I remember one time we played strip poker with an older boy from around the block. Halfway through the game he said, "You guys just want to see my dick, don't you?" He unzipped his pants, pulled down his underwear, and gave us a good look. It was much bigger than any of ours, and had lots of dark hair around it.

I remember a crowded birthday party for Patrick Merla, during a snowstorm, at an apartment on Washington Mews. I remember sitting on the staircase, smoking, and Joe towering over me telling me how attractive I looked in my black sweater.

I remember being afraid of getting a hard-on in the locker room.

I remember two boys wrestling on a gray mat, surrounded by the whole gym class. Suddenly one of the wrestlers "popped a boner." I remember how stunned everyone was. Then the whispers and snickers. I remember how embarrassed I felt for that boy.

I remember sitting through my high school chemistry class with a hard-on. Trying to concentrate on the chart of the elements, rather than the jocks all around me. Hoping none of them would see the bulge in my pants. And that it would "go down" before the bell rang.

I remember receiving a letter from Joe that said, "I'd love to see you when you're in town next month. Can I take you to dinner? And why don't you bring a tooth-brush with you and plan on spending the night." I remember how excited and flattered I was, then how disappointed: when I got to New York, Joe had a cold and couldn't keep our date.

I remember standing against a wall at the Club Baths in San Francisco. In 1976. Wearing nothing but a skimpy white towel. I remember a guy walking right up to me, reaching under the towel, and grabbing my cock. I remember how impressed I was by his directness, how I followed him to his cubicle. I remember having sex with him again—once at his place, once at mine. I remember that we sniffed Locker Room when we came.

I remember going on a secret date with my roommate's boyfriend. We drank a bottle of red wine at the beach, then made out on a couch in his sister's apartment. After we'd started having sex, I dramatically stood up, dressed, and left. The next day, he showed up and said, "What shall I call you now? 'Darling'?"

I remember pausing in the middle of sex with a guy to smoke a cigarette. He was insulted. But I needed a rest because our lovemaking was so intense.

I remember giving a reading with Lyn Hejinian at St. Mark's Church. It was a somber, humorless audience (mostly hers). But every time I looked up from my poems, I saw Joe's face in the center of the room, beaming handsomely at me.

A Regret

Kurt, early
twenties. Met
him after
an AA
meeting in
Silverlake
(November,
eighty-five).
I remem-
ber standing
with him up-
stairs, in the
clubhouse, how
I checked his
body out.
But not who
approached whom.
Or what we
talked about
before we
leaned against
my car and
kissed, under
that tarnished
L.A. moon.
Drove to my
place and un-
dressed him in
the dark. He
was smaller
than me. I
couldn't keep
my hands off
his ass. Next
morning, smoked
till he woke,

took him back.
He thanked me
sweetly. I
couldn't have
said what I
wanted, though
must have known.
Drove home and
put him in
a poem
("November")
I was at
the end of.

Later that
day it rained
(I know from
the poem).

After Neruda

When will the pastry learn
to take rejection well?

Why do certain cookies
stubbornly stick to the sheet?

What do Oscar winners do
without their awards, in heaven?

Shouldn't all jewelry be edible
that leaves a stain on the skin?

A Poet's Death

Rachel Sherwood
1954-1979

"What can you say about a twenty-five-year-old girl who died?"
—Erich Segal, *Love Story*

The first time we talked was in the rooftop
cafeteria at Cal State Northridge.
Misplaced poets, we sat amidst a crop
of clean-cut freshmen while, round the college,
smog-smudged San Fernando Valley beckoned,
panoramic and bland. I'd just returned
from my debauched year up north—sad, drunken
sex at the baths, in dark parks. You still yearned
for St. David's, your stint as a foreign
exchange student. In Wales, something fearless
woke you up: you drank, wrote, fucked. Now, stuck in
the suburbs, we talked poets, punk rock. This
was the late seventies, disco's zenith.
We both wanted to look like Patti Smith.

We both wanted to look like Patti Smith
on her *Horses* album: disheveled, pale,
thin, intense. You were scanning Meredith's
"Modern Love" for British Lit. I thought stale
anyone before Sexton. You laughed, threw
back your head. I puffed a Marlboro Light.
In truth, you were too hearty, and I too
uptight, to do punk. I praised, as twilight
dimmed the gray valley, a poem you'd read
at the student reading: a pitcher cracks,
foreshadows a car crash. The skyline bled
behind you. I'd also read that night—racked
with stage fright, trembling uncontrollably.
You seemed at ease, more confident than me.

You seemed at ease, more confident than me,
more independent. Lived on Amigo
Avenue with a roommate, a moody
science major; and your alter ego,
a tomcat named Baby Tubbs. Still at home,
I had no wheels. You drove a battered white
hatchback full of newspapers, beer cans, comb,
brush, books—half wastebasket, half purse. One night
early on, we split a fifth of scotch, spread
your tarot cards on the living room floor.
You predicted long life for me, then said
of yourself: "I *might* make twenty-five." Your
roommate walked by, shot a look. Later, I
passed out beneath Lord Byron's watchful eye.

Passed out beneath Lord Byron's watchful eye—
the poster tacked above your secondhand
couch—I dreamt I was falling down the side
of a mountain, a scarecrow, twisted and
limp, limbs ripped, bouncing from rock to rock. On
every wall an idol: Toulouse-Lautrec
cancan in kitchen, young Chatterton's wan
figure over your desk. Shuffling the deck,
you asked the same question, drew the same black
card: Death. Together we consulted all
your oracles: Ouija board, zodiac,
I Ching, palm, a fickle Magic 8 Ball.
Hoping for more time, you inquired, believed
like a convict praying for a reprieve.

Like a convict praying for a reprieve,
you were more alive than the complacent
suburbanites I despised. Drunk and peeved
at the world, I started an argument
that ended with you hurling a full Coors
at me as I fumed down your stairs. Four weeks
passed before we spoke, a rift I endured
by writing a poem about the freak-
ish night a black cloud followed us—we lit
candles, toasted oblivion. Battle
scarred, we entered the undergraduate
poetry contest at Northridge. Daniel
Halpern guest judged . . . or was it May Swenson?
After your death, I'd be happy you won.

What can you say about a twenty-five-
year-old girl who died? That as a child she
loved horses. And dogs. And cats. That Monty
Python made her laugh. That she was alive
to the disruptions of her time. That she
liked Byron, Rod Stewart, Mozart, Waugh, Poe,
Keats, the Cars. That she lived on Amigo
and was my friend. That she once threw her keys
in anger; once threw a *New Yorker*, shout-
ing "I hate John Ashbery!" And that she
once, after a speed- and scotch-fueled orgy—
Some Girls blasting, her last boyfriend passed out
beside us—straddled, rode me like a horse.
Rachel, can I say this: your cunt felt coarse.

After your death, I'd be happy you won
the contest—at least you had that. "Don't turn
on me," you pleaded. Losing wasn't fun,
but I couldn't begrudge you your prize. Burned
out from an abortion, a vicious bite—
a German shepherd lunged at your nose, slit
its tip—and a violent unrequit-
ed affair with your "Don J," a closet
case obsessed with Kerouac, you spoke of
making a change. By then it was summer:
Blondie on the car radio, Fourth of
July, craving fireworks. I remember
headlights; reaching for the steering wheel, you.
Next thing I knew, I woke in ICU.

Next thing I knew, I woke in ICU:
machines beeping around me, doctors and
nurses hovering in an eerie blue
light. Tube down my throat, I scrawled, with bruised hand,
your name, question mark. My sister was steered
in, wept to tell you were dead. The night they
moved me to a private room, you appeared,
pulsating white presence, in the hallway
outside my door. "I'm all right," you said, "You
don't have to worry about me." I'd lie
there in traction for six weeks, almost two
decades ago, a ghost that fell from my
own scarecrow dream, numb to that deadly drop.
The first time we talked was on a rooftop.

January 27 – March 10, 1999

To Tim Dlugos

That time you said Tom (regarding his stealing and selling
Ginsberg and Schuyler manuscripts to buy drugs)
had more reparations to make than Germany
after the war, you laughed your inimitable laugh:
self-satisfied, infectious. I sat rapt on my end of the line.
Now you're dead fifteen years, who once broke down
and confessed to Raymond, after a night at the baths,
your helpless addiction to unprotected sex. Update:
Eileen got a teaching job in San Diego. Dennis is
in Paris with a Russian boyfriend, Brad still looks thirty,
Tom is priest of a parish on Long Island. Ira and I split
up, and I left New York: teach poetry at an arts college
in the South Loop in Chicago. Turn my students
onto your work. Live north of downtown, on West
Hollywood Ave. (you'll never escape it, I can hear you
say, Hollywood is your state of mind) in Andersonville,
an old Swedish neighborhood full of gay men my age.

I'm at my computer thinking of your last days, how one
afternoon on G-9, sitting with you in awkward silence,
you asked point-blank: "Why did Dennis drop me?"
I stammered something about rivalry over a boy, afraid
to tell you, for some reason (you'd been sober many years),
that how you'd drunkenly lashed out during that rivalry
was the most accurate explanation. Then: "You've gained weight."
An uncharacteristically cranky moment, my friend, in an
otherwise grace-filled death. "I'll lose it," I said. And have.
Yesterday, walking home from the gym at dusk, I was struck
by the sky: a color you, who celebrated such nuances,
would have appreciated: Popsicle blue. Tim, I can still hear
your laugh, the closeness of your voice when you'd call,
late at night, to read a new poem or to relish the indiscretions
of others: "He's been crossed off guest lists I didn't know existed."
Nursing a ten-year crush, I was always reticent, let you—so smart
and so sharp—take the lead. I think I could keep up with you now.

James Schuyler

I went to his sixty-sixth birthday
dinner: sixteen years ago this past
November. I remember that it was at
Chelsea Central (his favorite restaurant:
great steaks) on 10th Avenue, and
that Ashbery was there, and a few
others, including Joe, impeccably
dressed and gracious, who picked up
what must have been (I thought
at the time) an exorbitant bill.

I remember him saying more than
once, "Joe always picks up the bill,"
then smiling a slightly wicked smile.

Sitting with him (those excruciating
silences!) in his room at the Chelsea,
my eyes would wander from his book-
shelves (*The Portrait of a Lady* stood out)
to the pan of water on the radiator
to the records strewn on the floor
to some scraggly plants (ivy? herbs?)
in ceramic pots at the base of the French
doors that opened to the balcony and
balustrade and sound of traffic on 23rd
Street six floors below. He read me
"White Boat, Blue Boat" shortly after he
wrote it, and a poem about Brook Benton
singing "Rainy Night in Georgia" that
didn't make it into his *Last Poems*, though
I remember thinking it beautiful. He
complained, in a letter to Tom, about
how much I smoked, and how emotional
I'd get during movies: he must have been
referring to *Field of Dreams* (he had a yen
for Kevin Costner). When he took me

to see *L'Atalante*, a film he loved, I was
bored. Once, we took the subway (he
hadn't ridden it in years) to the Frick;
I remember admiring Romney's Lady
Hamilton. It hurt that he didn't invite
me to the dinner after his Dia reading
or to the reception after his reading at the
92nd Street Y, though he did, at the latter,
read "Mood Indigo," dedicated to me.
When he said my name from the stage,
Joan and Eileen, sitting to my left, turned
and stared at me; frozen by the enormity
of the moment, I couldn't look back.
When he came to a reading I gave at
St. Mark's, Raymond impressed upon
me what an honor it was: Jimmy didn't
go to many poetry readings. What else
is there to say? That when I visited him
at St. Vincent's the day before he died
Darragh said, "He likes to hear gossip."
So I said, "Eileen and I are talking again."
That at his funeral I sat alone (Ira couldn't
come); that that was the loneliest feeling
in the world. That afterwards Doug said
"You look so sad." How should I have
looked, Doug! And that a year after he
died, I dreamt I saw him in the lobby of
the Chelsea Hotel. He was wearing a
hospital shift and seemed to have no
muscle control over his face—like in inten-
sive care after his stroke. He saw me
and said, "It's nice to see some familiar
faces." I approached him, but he
disappeared.

Nature Poem

Till the Clouds Roll By
A Patch of Blue

How Green Was My Valley
Splendor in the Grass

The Petrified Forest
The River of No Return

Lilies of the Field
The Bad Seed

A Tree Grows in Brooklyn
Autumn Leaves

Lost Horizon
Gone With the Wind

Penelope

Penelope was a housewife
    So bored she planned a prank:
Despite her Central Park highlife,
    She robbed her husband's bank.

Like a rewound Cinderella,
    She went from princess to hag;
Held a toy gun as the teller
    Stuffed sixty grand in her bag.

She asked: "Which way is the ladies' room?"
    The stunned teller pointed left.
Inside, she donned a new costume
    While sirens broadcast the theft.

The bank was sheer pandemonium,
    Her husband's worst nightmare.
He led police to the powder room,
    The perpetrator's lair.

A redhead in a chic yellow suit
    Flew from the john and cried:
"The old lady in there said she'll shoot!"
    Then cheerfully wiggled outside.

The cops crept in, armed for their task,
    But found no one at all . . .
Just a plain frock, gray wig, and mask
    Hung in a bathroom stall.

As the cab sped up Park Avenue,
    Penelope ducked in back;
Freed brunette curls from her fake red do,
    Changed clothes from yellow to black.

"Please drop me at Bergdorf Goodman."
    She brushed a mischievous tress.

She pranced past the uniformed doorman
    And bought a new cocktail dress.

*

The first few scenes, in a nutshell,
    Of the mid-sixties flick
About a madcap mademoiselle,
    A zany light-fingered chick.

The script, based on a slim novel
    By E. V. Cunningham,
Was picked up by a young mogul
    Who produced for MGM.

His name was Arthur Loew, Jr.,
    Heir to the theater chain.
He envisioned a moneymaker
    That would also entertain.

In terms of box-office cachet,
    No one in Hollywood
Could touch his former fiancée,
    Superstar Natalie Wood.

Loew had wooed Nat years earlier,
    After a torrid affair
With cad Warren Beatty left her
    On the verge of despair.

Arthur prevented a tailspin,
    Helped Natalie to forget;
Consoled her when she failed to win
    The golden statuette.

Though their engagement fell apart,
    Their friendship stayed intact.
If she'd accept the leading part,
    His picture would get backed.

She listened to his lavish pitch
  And seemed somewhat impressed.
There was one unexpected glitch:
  The actress was depressed.

Reviewers had been uncivil
  Towards her last two attempts.
They'd dismissed *Daisy* as drivel,
  Heaped *Property* with contempt.

A fling with a married director
  Had only brought remorse.
She ended it when the traitor
  Refused to file for divorce.

Loew convinced her *Penelope*
  Would be the perfect thing—
Better than psychotherapy—
  To mitigate love's sting.

Her agents advised against it.
  The script, they said, was weak.
Natalie, weary of pundits,
  Ignored their wise critique.

If the screenplay lacked inspiration,
  The deal she struck was shrewd:
Three-quarters of a cool million
  Would surely improve her mood.

Because the star's fee was so high
  And their budget far from vast,
Producers were forced to rely
  On a less famous cast.

Scots actor Ian Bannen played
  Nat's spouse as bumbling suit.
Pre-*Columbo* Peter Falk portrayed
  A sleuth in pursuit of the loot.

Costume designer Edith Head
    Concocted "schizoid" clothes:
For kooky thief, outlandish threads;
    For housewife, frills and bows.

Arthur Hiller, hired to direct,
    Cried "Cut!" and coddled his star:
"I think you're resisting this project.
    Your wit isn't up to par."

Distressed, the actress broke out in
    Hives after every scene.
She dreamed she plunged down a mountain
    In a brakeless limousine.

Penelope soon proved to be
    The nadir of her career.
The public would not flock to see
    A film full of false cheer.

Both word of mouth and bad reviews
    Blamed Natalie for the dud.
Adverse press and poor revenues
    Quickly chill Tinseltown blood.

Celebs as big as Wood must rake
    In equally big dough.
Not even she could afford to make
    Three failures in a row.

Ensconced in deepest Beverly Hills,
    The movie star took to bed.
A steady diet of red pills
    Numbed overwhelming dread.

Those closest to the actress were
    Concerned about her plight.
Her therapist placed himself at her
    Disposal day and night.

Ex-secretary Mart Crowley
    Resided on the grounds.
From guest house he was poised to see
    That Natalie would rebound.

Mart's recompense for holding Nat's hand
    Was a poolside place to stay
Where he typed at *Boys in the Band*,
    His soon-to-be-smash gay play.

B-actress sibling Lana Wood
    Set rivalry aside,
Endeavoring as best she could
    To lure big sis outside.

When a table at La Scala
    Failed to rouse Nat from bed,
Lana had their renowned pasta
    Delivered to her instead.

Bad times brought the sisters closer
    Than they'd been in recent years.
They talked as they had as youngsters,
    Divulging secret fears.

Natalie was worried that as
    A woman she'd lost her knack.
How could she be desired en masse
    Yet lack a man in the sack?

One afternoon a visitor
    Appeared out of her past:
Warren Beatty, former suitor,
    With a pet project to cast.

To interest filmic financiers,
    Whom he'd pitched far and wide,
He sought a pre-eminent player,
    A Bonnie for his Clyde.

Indifferent to Warren's plea,
    Natalie said "No thanks."
She'd had, due to *Penelope,*
    Enough of robbing banks.

Ironically, the outlaw tale
    Would've put Nat back on top.
But the synopsis sounded stale;
    She figured it would flop.

Mart heard raised voices coming from
    The main part of the house.
He knew, though classically handsome,
    Warren was at heart a louse.

As Beatty sped off in his sports car,
    Natalie was morose.
She calmly walked to her boudoir
    And took an overdose.

Just before she lost consciousness,
    Nat was suddenly scared.
She called out, crawled nearly lifeless . . .
    Mart found her on the stairs.

The first thing that he thought to do
    Was dial "Dr. John."
Nat's shrink told Mart to rush her to
    Cedars of Lebanon.

John met them in ER pronto
    And had her stomach pumped.
Then admitted her incognito
    So reporters would be stumped.

While therapist and movie star
    Fought for an hour or more,
Mart and two hospital staffers
    Kept watch outside the door.

Both did a great deal of shouting
    About Nat's downward trend—
Actress doubting, doctor touting
    The life she'd tried to end.

Since John insisted Natalie stay
    In Cedars overnight,
Mart hatched a plan that, the next day,
    Would aid her in her flight:

In old clothes that would be supplied
    By younger sister Lana,
They'd sneak her out past press that vied
    Like gossip-starved piranhas.

That night as she was ushered in
    With Natalie's disguise,
Lana began to choke up when
    She met her sister's eyes.

Nat's unbrushed hair was hanging down
    Into her puffy face.
She looked as if she'd almost drowned
    In her drenched pillowcase.

Her tiny swollen body wore
    A loose hospital gown.
The shining star the world adored
    Had plummeted straight down.

Lana leaned over and kissed her
    Like she never had before.
"I didn't," Natalie whispered,
    "Want to live anymore."

The actress sadly looked away
    As Lana took her hand.
"And now you do?" she managed to say—
    Less question than demand.

The two sat in silence for a while
    Until Nat finally moved.
She turned toward Lana and weakly smiled.
    "Yes," she said, "Now I do."

*

Within three years she'd score a hit
    With a group sex parody.
A percentage of the profits
    Would set her up nicely.

She'd take a break from the glamour grind,
    Put acting on the shelf.
Instead she'd focus on her mind
    And get to know herself.

Luck would grant her a second shot
    With husband number one:
She and R.J. would retie the knot
    And astonish everyone.

Together they'd raise a family,
    Their happiness airtight
Till their unplanned date with destiny
    At sea one moonless night.

As for the fate of Penelope,
    The film you'll have to see.
It's broadcast periodically
    On Turner Classic Movies.

Sonnet

The day she died, my mother divided
up her jewelry, placed each piece in Dixie
cups (on which my father had written, with
magic marker, the names of her children
and grandchildren): her aunt's pearls, her mother-
in-law's topaz and amethysts, her own
mother's plain gold cross. Earlier, I'd held
a mirror while she put on her lipstick
(Summer Punch) and ran a comb through what was
left of her hair. She stared at the gray strands
in her hand—not with sadness, but as fact.
When she placed the last ring in the last cup,
she looked up at me and said, "We never
have enough time to enjoy our treasures."

Doll Memorial Service

[*for Elaine Equi*]

There are many ways
a fashion doll can
die: chewed limbs, split
neck, ponytail snipped to
the hair plugs. This
beauty perished because her
owner left her "pearl"
earrings in their holes:
stored in the dark
for twenty-five years,
metal interacted with vinyl
and turned half her
face green—wicked witch
in profile—a condition
known as "green ear."
And isn't it right
that they should die.
This lovely elicited angry
indifference in a tomboy.
This gal incited rivalry
in sister, jealousy in
best friend. This is
the charmer responsible for
inspiring the ache—eternal,
inevitable—in an introverted
boy. Age has robbed
her of her face
paint. And this is
the stunner I bought
at a doll shop
an hour before my
mother died. Though I'd
fly the doll home,
dress and display her,
I knew I wouldn't

keep her long. Sold
to the highest bidder
on eBay, she's out
there somewhere, loose in
the world, death set
in her side-glance,
on tight red lips.

Classic Layer Cakes

> *Mother is gone,*
> *only Things remain.*
> —Denise Levertov

9773 Comanche Ave. A pale yellow, ranch-style tract house in the suburbs of Los Angeles. White shutters. Decorative cast iron trellis (leaves and acorns), painted white, around the front porch. Dichondra. Gardenias. Ivy in the parkway, beginning to climb a Modesto Ash. Snapdragons in the flowerbeds. Bottlebrush in the backyard.

The phone number, when we moved there in the late fifties, was Dickens (DI) 9-1647. The prefix was later changed to 349.

Osso, Lassen, Winnetka, Plummer: the streets that boxed in our world.

My mother in her frilled apron, dusting and vacuuming; sweeping and mopping; rinsing, scouring, scrubbing. Driving her station wagon to the supermarket. Pushing the cart. Crossing each item off her shopping list. Her large, slightly loopy handwriting slanting towards the right. Perusing *The Brand-Name Calorie Counter* at the check-out stand. Folding her receipt and Green Stamps into her purse. Pulling into the driveway. Unloading the brown grocery bags, setting them on the speckled linoleum in her pink kitchen. Emptying them, folding them, flattening them, stacking them.

What treats she'd take out of those bags: Wheat Thins, Triscuits, Oreos, Nilla Wafers, Bugles, Sno Balls, Twinkies, Cheez-Its, Ritz. Laura Scudder's potato chips came in twin-paks, in big red, yellow, and brown striped bags. After my mother died, at a store near her home, those colors caught my eye. I bought a package, folded and saved it (threw away the chips). The expiration date, stamped on the bag, is June 23, 1996.

the fork marks in her peanut butter cookies

her pink and light green Depression glass
her collection of souvenir spoons
The Ray Conniff Singers
Sing Along with Mitch

the milk glass (hobnail, ruffled) in the Early American hutch
her German cuckoo clock

She sent away to Northern Paper Mills, makers of fine toilet tissue, for a set of
American Beauty Portraits: 11 x 14 prints of sweet little girls: one holding
daisies, one cuddling a kitten, one bundled up against the snow. Which she
framed and hung in the hall. There was also one of an infant peeking out of a
pink blanket.

My brother and I are outside, in the front yard, when it begins to rain. Soon it
is pouring. I find this exciting, dance around in my soaked clothes and then
lose myself in play: floating my Mickey Mouse pirate ship in the rushing river
the gutter has become. Pleased with ourselves, we knock on the door—to surprise
my mother. But she is furious. She grabs and undresses us, wraps us in towels,
and makes us dry off in front of the fireplace.

So much to be afraid of: earthquake, mudslide, wildfire, plane crash, train
wreck, car accident, Communism, nuclear war, riots, gas shortage, Skylab,
burglar, rapist, kidnapper, mass murderer, botulism, polio, rabies, tetanus, lockjaw,
gangrene, infection, germs, sirens, black widow, rattlesnake, calories, high
cholesterol, heart attack, cancer.

PTA meetings. Tupperware parties. Den Mother. "Avon calling."

One year, she threw a surprise birthday party for my father. Invited neighbors
and some of his Lockheed colleagues. It never happened again; my father
didn't like being surprised. I remember shish kabob skewers on the barbeque on
the back patio and a huge brandy snifter filled with cantaloupe, honeydew, and
watermelon balls.

I also remember a shower she gave for one of her friends. There were dishes
full of mixed nuts and pastel pillow mints, and candied almonds wrapped in
tulle and tied with curling ribbon. They played a game where each woman,
blindfolded and using a spoon, had to lift as many cotton balls as she could
from that same brandy snifter.

My mother lying on the couch in front of the TV, watching the late show,
crying. *Since You Went Away*: Claudette Colbert and her daughters (Jennifer Jones
and Shirley Temple) holding down the home front. *The Fighting Sullivans*: five

brothers, stationed on the same battleship during World War II, perish together. Family tragedy: my mother's nineteen-year-old cousin George also died at Guadalcanal.

Years later she tells me her deepest secret: when they were children, George molested her.

her suffering, her experience, her emotion

After the war ended, her mother, Marguerite, died of leukemia. My mother was fourteen. A family photo taken during Marguerite's illness: my mother's angry expression. "I didn't want that picture taken."

Moments before she died, Marguerite cried out: "George is calling me."

Imitation of Life: the scene where Sarah Jane (Susan Kohner), full of remorse and grief, throws herself on her mother's coffin.

Her migraine headaches. Her weight problem. The mornings she slept late, unable to get out of bed.

In the mid-eighties, my parents were traveling in their motor home. Parked at a campground one night, they became friendly with a couple their age, sat talking over drinks. The woman, when the subject of Rock Hudson, gay men and AIDS came up, said: "What do they expect us to do?" "They expect us to help them," my mother replied.

In the previous passage I initially wrote "mother home" instead of "motor home."

My father once said she loved children and the elderly, but wasn't fond of many people in between.

Her first breakdown: she woke up in the middle of the night, looked out her bedroom window, and saw—hanging in the backyard—a pair of golden drapes.

My mother's burden, all her adult life: my father's anger. His daily outbursts, his constant belittling. It eventually wore her down, defeated her. How many times did I hear her say, in the middle of one of his fits: "Shhh! What will the neighbors think." She once told me he never showed his temper until they were married. After she died, my father said that when they were newlyweds, my mother got so angry she threw a cast iron ashtray at him. It really hurt—he walked around the block in pain. His anecdote made me laugh. *Good for her.*

A phone call from my father. "Your mother has cancer." "Where?" "Down there." Ira and I spend Christmas in Paris as planned, but it is cold and rainy, and I am depressed. I lie awake in our hotel room late one night watching a film in which Santa Claus battles the Devil—in Spanish, with French subtitles. Unable to enjoy the surreal juxtapositions, I long to understand what is being said.

How in the midst of her illness, returning from the hospital, she bribed an ambulance driver to stop at McDonald's. How when I was in high school and she'd pick me up at the library on weeknights, we often drove through McDonald's on the way home. "Don't tell your father." How it used to tick me off that she'd pick at my French fries. "Why didn't you get your own?"

When we were sick she'd bring us Campbell's chicken noodle soup, saltines, and ginger ale on a TV tray. A rerun of *I Love Lucy* was also medicinal.

Thinking it the first of many such trips I'd have to take, I flew from New York to Los Angeles. Rented a car and drove to central California, where my parents had retired. She was in an extended care facility in Santa Maria. The first thing she said to me was: "Did you bring me a poem?" Later, waking and find- ing me sitting there, she said: "This can't be fun for you." "It's why I came, to see you." At one point, when I was telling her about my teaching, my writing, she pronounced: "It's taken you a long time, but you've come up in the world."

How, before she died, decades seemed to drop away. She looked younger, prettier, than she had in years.

her Kleenex tissues
her Aqua Net hairspray
her Jergens lotion
her Camay soap
her Calgon bath oil beads
her Clairol shampoo
her Avon lipstick samples: tiny white plastic tubes
her jar of Topaze cream (a yellow jewel embedded in its lid)

The morning she died, she called my father from the hospice. Said she'd thought she was going to die the night before. Thought that she was hemorrhaging. And that her mother, Marguerite, was coming for her.

I was eight months sober when she had her first breakdown. My mother was convinced that their house had been bugged, that their neighbor, a redheaded woman, was the leader of a suburban drug ring. There may have been some truth to this. One night when I visited my parents (they were still on Comanche Ave.), the tires on my car were slashed. I went to see my mother when she was in the psych ward at Northridge Hospital. I remember almost nothing—only that we sat together and talked. That Christmas, in the middle of preparing the holiday meal, my mother, fed up with my father's nagging, asked me to take her "anywhere." We drove up to Chatsworth Park, sat looking at the lights of the San Fernando Valley. "Do you think someone's looking out for you?" she asked. "You mean like God or a Higher Power or something?" "Yes." "Yes," I said, "I do believe that."

I spent the morning with her, helping her divide up her jewelry. I took a break for lunch, drove up the coast to a doll store I'd found in the Yellow Pages. I remember having a funny feeling as I drove back. When I walked in the house, the phone was ringing. It was my father: "Get here quick!" The wildest ride of my life: doing 90 on 101, in my mother's Taurus, thinking "Wait!" The dreamlike sensation of watching myself from outside myself: This wasn't really happening. I pulled into the parking lot. As I walked towards the hospice, I saw a woman (a nurse?) out of the corner of my eye, pointing and gesturing that I should run. So I ran. My sister pulled me into the room.

What I said to my mother as she was dying:
"Thank you for being my mother. I love you."
"You're onto the next step of the journey. God be with you."
"You've done a good job, Mom. You can let go now."

I saw the nurse look at her watch, heard her say "time of death." Then I crumpled beside the bed, sobbing.

My father said he cried once, while she was dying. "That's the only time I'm going to cry." I remembered my mother telling me that she'd tried to get him, after he'd retired, to go with her to a therapist. He'd refused, saying he was too set in his ways, wasn't about to change now.

I remember thinking: Now I know what a dead person looks like.

Later I'm told that after she hemorrhaged she yelled: "Oh God, take me now!"

The house my parents retired to was also pale yellow. When my father and I went to Costco to buy food for the reception after the funeral, he insisted that the cake be pale yellow, like her houses.

My father says it was all the sodas, all the Cokes, that killed her.

I remember the two framed ballerinas in her lavender bedroom. I remember the soft light and silence when, alone in the house, I'd intrude on my parents' privacy: explore their walk-in closet, riffle through drawers. Her dresses and ruffled slips, her clip-on costume earrings. On the dresser: ceramic figurines: Pinky and Blue Boy, the Virgin Mary. In a bedside drawer: her rosary and prayer book, and a bundle of her and my father's love letters (tied with a white ribbon).

A day or two after the funeral, before I went back to New York, my sister pulled me aside and handed me my parents' love letters. "You should keep these," she whispered, "Dad will just throw them out." I did keep them for a while, but couldn't bring myself to read them. When I sold my papers to Fales Library at NYU, I included the letters, still tied in ribbon. I remember the air of mystery, of secrecy these letters had when I was a child; that they still have.

My mother in the rear view mirror, waving and undoubtedly crying, at visit's end, as I drive away.

A month after my mother's death, I have a phone session with Helen. She tells me my mother was ready to go, that her mother, Marguerite, and a friend were there to greet her. She says that my mother isn't coming back right away, that she is undergoing a process of "soul healing." She can do this in the Ethers; she doesn't have to be here on Earth. Helen hears healing sounds. Musical healing. Healing at the deepest level of being. My mother will begin, when she's ready, a whole new cycle, one of pleasure, peacefulness, and beauty. She also says that my mother and Marguerite are together, and that they're aware of the conversation Helen and I are having.

Most reincarnational philosophies teach that a long period of celestial rest usual-
ly intervenes between incarnations—a time for assimilating the harvest of life's
experiences. Then, refreshed and invigorated, the individual returns, not in sad-
ness and despair but, as childhood attests, in eager joyousness to undertake a new
adventure in learning and growing.

What I had them put in her coffin: a lucky penny and two fortunes: "You will
be singled out for promotion" and "There is a prospect of a thrilling time ahead
for you."

Helen said the woman I saw out of the corner of my eye, who encouraged me
to run, was my mother. She wanted to make sure I'd be there at the end.

Time of death: 6:05 p.m., Wednesday, May 8, 1996. Insult to injury: that she
should die right before Mother's Day. My father, as we made the funeral
arrangements, said: "I guess it won't be much of a Christmas this year."

One of the ironies of her death: that I should develop a closer relationship with
my father. How he asked me to be his executor: of the four children, he said, I
am the one who can communicate. He's been supportive of my poetry, and I
see that he is proud of what I've accomplished, though when I was younger it
seemed he did all he could to thwart my efforts to be a writer.

In the weeks before Christmas, my mother hides presents around the house:
under beds, in cupboards and closets. I am given to snooping; she tells me not
to poke around. I find a gift for my brother—the *Combat!* board game—in the
hamper in my father's bathroom. Unable to contain myself, I let her know I'm
in on the secret. Instead of welcoming me as her conspirator, she slaps me
across the face.

Things she put in our Christmas stockings: candy canes, oranges, batteries,
maple leaf candies, yo-yos, pennies, socks.

How she always wanted Christmas to be perfect; how it was always spoiled by
my father's tirades. Decorating the tree: boxes of ornaments, strands of colored
lights, on the living room floor. Christmas morning: ribbon and wrapping
paper everywhere. He resented the mess.

her special holiday china: Franciscan Desert Rose

One year, instead of tinsel, she covered the tree with angel hair. I remember her saying to be careful, when I tried to help, because it could cut your fingers, get in your eyes. The fact that something so pretty could also be dangerous could not have been lost on me.

I wish I could do this memory better.

Using sponges, dipped in colored Glass Wax, to stencil the windows with snowflakes, reindeer, candles, wreaths. Watching her arrange her cookies—drizzled, sprinkled, powdered, frosted—on the three-tiered serving tray. Gazing at the Sears Christmas catalog, pretending *not* to look at the pages of girls' toys: Barbie and her friends; metal two-story dollhouses; child-size cardboard kitchens and supermarkets; play food; Suzy Homemaker vacuum cleaner and ironing board; cake mix sets with electric ovens.

Come into Miss Cookie's Kitchen. I purchased, on eBay, this 1962 Colorforms set. My sisters must have had it, because I distinctly remember how you could open Miss Cookie's refrigerator, oven, and cupboards and press her yellow teapot, her green cake, and her pink milk bottle inside. Taped to the upper right-hand corner of the box is the original gift tag—a smiling Santa face. Printed across his white beard is the name Patti.

Christmas, 1963: my sisters receive Deluxe Reading's Barbie-scale Dream Kitchen. Even while opening my own presents, I can't keep my eyes off of it. "Santa" had opened the box and set up those colorful plastic appliances: pink sink and brown dishwasher (both with running water), yellow oven (with rotating turkey and glowing red burners), turquoise refrigerator (with swing-out shelves). Countless accessories: dishes, silverware, utensils, food. Three decades later, it will take me a number of pre-eBay years to piece together a complete set, mostly by scouring doll shows. Precious: the plastic cakes (with hairline cracks), the ice cube and egg trays, the tiny boxes of sugar, crackers, and lemon cookies.

August, 2005: I visit my friend Bec in Largo, Florida. My first night there we sit up late, talking, admiring her Barbie collection. From a closet she produces a Deluxe Reading Kitchen, never played with, in its original box. It's a hard feeling to describe: confronting what I desired and couldn't have, in such pristine condition—brand new, as if it had been transported via a time machine. Thrilling, and yet sad. After looking at it, I say: "My mother couldn't have known how important this stuff was to me." Bec agrees. I feel my mother's presence in the room. The next morning, Bec says: "I felt that your mother was with us last night." "I did too," I tell her.

A turning point in my collecting: when I realized I had bought myself every Barbie item my mother had bought my sisters.

Ira, Dianne, and I wander around the Chelsea flea market. I spot an old Sears catalog and start flipping through it. Ira comes over to look at it with me. The dealer, a woman in her thirties, says we can buy, but not look at it. "How can I tell if I want to buy it unless I look at it?" The woman reaches for the catalog and slides it away from us. "Cunt," I say. I look back as we make our way through the market, can see how agitated she is. We have to pass her table on the way out. She charges up to me and says: "What would your mother say?" Ira and Dianne are afraid I'll lose it, since my mother has just died. But I don't respond. "She's right," I say to them. And feel the reprimand has come straight from my mother.

After she died, I bought, at an antique mall, a stack of magazines from the early sixties. *Better Homes and Gardens. Family Circle. McCall's.* Late at night I'd look through them—at pictures of housewives in kitchens and dining rooms; at ads for laundry detergent and floor wax; at recipes for Rice Krispie treats and pumpkin pie—and cry.

My mother in her apron, baking. My mother combining, mixing, blending, and stirring. My mother flattening the dough on the breadboard with her rolling pin. My mother squeezing the handle of her flour sifter. My mother kneading, blanching, creaming, and whipping. My mother pouring tomato aspic into a Jell-O mold. My mother measuring, folding, removing, and filling. My mother greasing the cookie sheet. My mother placing paper cupcake liners in her muffin pan. My mother beating, sprinkling, crimping, and tinting. My mother cutting the dough into strips for a lattice crust. My mother consulting her *Betty Crocker Cookbook.* My mother using a spatula to evenly spread frosting to the edge of the first layer. My mother frosting the sides. My mother applying more frosting with free, easy strokes. My mother spreading frosting on top, making swirls with the back of a spoon.

Angel Food. Pineapple Upside-Down. Lemon Chiffon. German Chocolate. Red Velvet. Classic White.

Licking the last streaks of batter from the bowl, or one of the beaters when she finished whipping the cream. After making a pie, she'd transform remnants of dough into "Roly-Polies": strips sprinkled with cinnamon and sugar, then rolled and baked. Through the glass oven door, I'd watch them puff up and turn brown.

gardenias from the front yard floating in a shallow bowl on the kitchen table

A photograph taken the day I graduated from Nobel Junior High. Northridge, California. June, 1968. I stand, stiffly, in front of the entrance on Tampa Ave., in suit and tie, squinting at the camera (my father), trying to smile. My mother stands a few feet to the right, facing me. She wears a sleeveless floral print dress. Her hair has been done. In her left hand she holds the commencement program and her purse. Her right hand is raised to her throat, in proud excitement. She is smiling broadly.

Last time I visited my father, there wasn't a trace of my mother in the house. He'd gotten rid of everything. Given most of her belongings to my sisters. Saved a few things for me, in a small box on the top shelf of a closet in a guest room. The Tiffany china (tulips) I'd sent her from New York several Christmases, a couple pieces of her cut glass.

I miss my mother.

Searching eBay for *The Sound of Hollywood:* The Medallion Strings performing themes from *The Apartment, The Sundowners, A Summer Place, Spellbound, The Alamo, Never on Sunday, Midnight Lace*. Staring at the photo of the blue-on-blue album cover and deciding not to bid. Enough to simply remember lying in front of the hi-fi in the living room, while she cleans or cooks in the kitchen, listening to those dramatic tunes.

After E.D. (#873)

The housewife's Vanity –
Holding her Style in place
Lips impressing a tissue
With prerequisite Red

Crumpled and discarded
As Beauty's Publication
Her necklace – Costume –
Party Dress – Expedient –

Queen Bee

[for Robyn Schiff]

"It's really not like me,"
says the timid cousin.

"Then you
be like the dress."

See how slyly
she removes her

sleep mask.
How maliciously

she swats the dolls
with her riding crop.

How she
gleefully destroys

the lives of those
around her.

O evil matriarch!
O wicked frock!

Hack, Hack, Sweet Has-Been

What Ever Happened to Baby Jane? is an excellent movie and well worth
    owning on DVD.
Bette Davis goes over the top as Jane Hudson, a former child star gone to seed.
She slouches around in a fright wig, bedroom slippers, and makeup that
    looks put on with a putty knife.
In a decaying Hollywood mansion, she tortures her crippled sister Blanche
    (Joan Crawford), once a screen idol.

Bette Davis goes over the top as Jane Hudson, a former child star gone to seed.
It's impossible to look away from her clownish chalk-white face.
In a decaying Hollywood mansion, she tortures her crippled sister Blanche
    (Joan Crawford), once a screen idol,
And deludes herself into believing she can make a theatrical comeback by
    reviving her old vaudeville act.

It's impossible to look away from Jane's clownish chalk-white face.
She sings her signature song from when she was a little girl, "I've Written a
    Letter to Daddy,"
And deludes herself into believing she can make a theatrical comeback by
    reviving her old vaudeville act.
But when she gets a look at herself in the mirror and sees what time and age
    have done to her, she screams.

She sings her signature song from when she was a little girl, "I've Written a
    Letter to Daddy."
Meanwhile, her wheelchair-bound sister is trapped upstairs.
When Jane gets a look at herself in the mirror and sees what time and age
    have done to her, she screams.
Hearing this, Blanche presses a buzzer in her room to see what has happened.

Her wheelchair-bound sister is trapped upstairs.
Blanche desperately tries to get away, but all avenues of escape are cut off by
    the deranged Jane.
Blanche presses a buzzer in her room.
Jane brings Blanche her lunch on a silver tray.

Blanche desperately tries to get away, but all avenues of escape are cut off by
the deranged Jane.
Crawford wisely underacts; if her performance isn't as showy as Davis's, it's
not any less accomplished.
Jane brings Blanche her lunch on a silver tray.
In one of the cinema's most macabre moments, Blanche lifts the cover off the
dish to find a dead parakeet.

Crawford wisely underacts; if her performance isn't as showy as Davis's, it's
not any less accomplished.
During production, the feud between these two divas was highly publicized.
In one of the cinema's most macabre moments, Blanche lifts the cover off the
dish to find a dead rat.
The real-life animosity makes for some compelling on-screen sibling rivalry.

During production, the feud between these two divas was highly publicized.
Davis had a Coke machine installed on the set to anger Crawford, whose late
husband was an executive at Pepsi.
The real-life animosity makes for some compelling on-screen sibling rivalry.
Davis's foot allegedly made contact with Crawford's head during a scene
where Baby Jane punts Blanche around the living room.

Davis had a Coke machine installed on the set to anger Crawford, whose late
husband was an executive at Pepsi.
Crawford insulted Davis's daughter, who appeared in a small role as the
teenager who lives next door to the Hudson sisters.
Davis's foot allegedly made contact with Crawford's head during a scene
where Baby Jane punts Blanche around the living room.
In retaliation, Crawford put weights in her pockets so that when Davis had to
drag Crawford's near-lifeless body she strained her back.

Crawford insulted Davis's daughter, who appeared in a small role as the
teenager who lives next door to the Hudson sisters.
Davis bitched to director Robert Aldrich about Crawford's drinking (both
women were alcoholics) and padded brassieres.
In retaliation, Crawford put weights in her pockets so that when Davis had to
drag Crawford's near-lifeless body she strained her back.
Despite their utter dislike for each other, the film was a critical and commercial
success and it revitalized their sagging careers.

Davis bitched to director Robert Aldrich about Crawford's drinking (both
    women were alcoholics) and padded brassieres.
Davis commanded a larger salary, Crawford a higher percentage of the gross.
Despite their utter dislike for each other, the film was a critical and commercial
    success and it revitalized their sagging careers.
Davis received her tenth and final Oscar nomination for her portrayal of Baby
    Jane.

Davis commanded a larger salary, Crawford a higher percentage of the gross.
They hoped to duplicate their success in a follow-up, again directed by Aldrich,
    called *Hush, Hush . . . Sweet Charlotte.*
Davis received her tenth and final Oscar nomination for her portrayal of Baby
    Jane.
Davis's torment of Crawford (who had campaigned against Davis's nomination)
    became so oppressive that Crawford feigned illness in order to get out of
    the production.

They hoped to duplicate their success in a follow-up, again directed by Aldrich,
    called *Hush, Hush . . . Sweet Charlotte,*
With Davis as the title character, a reclusive Southern belle accused of an axe
    murder.
On location in Louisiana, Davis's torment of Crawford became so oppressive
    that Crawford feigned illness and held up filming for weeks.
Eventually she was replaced by Olivia de Havilland.

With Davis as the shrieking Charlotte, a reclusive Southern belle accused of
    an axe murder,
Rafter-rattling overacting is the call of the day.
Crawford was replaced by Davis's friend Olivia de Havilland,
Who plays Charlotte's seemingly sweet-tempered cousin Miriam to the hilt.

Rafter-rattling overacting is the call of the day.
In a decaying plantation mansion, strange things start happening.
De Havilland plays the seemingly sweet-tempered Miriam to the hilt,
Intent upon driving Charlotte out of her mind and getting her mitts on the
    family fortune.

In a decaying plantation mansion, strange things start happening.
Awakened late at night by a haunting harpsichord, Charlotte finds her dead
  lover's disembodied hand.
Intent upon driving Charlotte out of her mind and getting her mitts on the
  family fortune,
Olivia de Havilland sends a severed head rolling down the staircase at Bette
  Davis.

Awakened late at night by a haunting harpsichord, Charlotte finds her dead
  lover's disembodied hand.
While not as tight as *Baby Jane, Charlotte* features some unforgettable moments,
  including a scene where de Havilland slaps Davis senseless
Then sends a severed head rolling down the staircase.
Many fans would rather have seen Crawford smack Davis across the face.

While not as tight as *Baby Jane, Charlotte* features some unforgettable moments,
  including a scene where de Havilland slaps Davis senseless
And viciously snarls, "Now will you shut your mouth!"
Many fans would rather have seen Crawford smack Davis across the face.
The film was another big hit, although Davis was miffed that one critic labeled
  her "Hollywood's *grande-dame* ghoul."

"Now will you shut your mouth!"
Reviewers with a yen for violence applauded the picture.
Davis was miffed that one critic labeled her "Hollywood's *grande-dame*
  ghoul."
Throughout the sixties, the names of Bette Davis and Joan Crawford were
  synonymous with horror movies.

Reviewers with a yen for violence applauded the picture.
This sparked a trend towards casting over-the-hill leading ladies in gothic
  horror flicks.
Throughout the sixties, the names of Bette Davis and Joan Crawford were
  synonymous with such movies.
Davis starred in *Dead Ringer* and *The Nanny* among others, and Crawford in
  gorier fare like *Strait-Jacket* and *Berserk!*

This sparked a trend towards casting over-the-hill leading ladies in gothic horror flicks.
Barbara Stanwyck, Tallulah Bankhead, and Joan Fontaine made forays in the genre.
Davis starred in *Dead Ringer* and *The Nanny* among others, and Crawford in gorier fare like *Strait-Jacket* and *Berserk!*
In *Strait-Jacket,* Crawford portrays a deranged woman who discovers her husband in bed with his lover and hacks their heads off.

Shelley Winters, Debbie Reynolds, and Geraldine Page made forays in the genre.
Crawford caused the most damage to her reputation by accepting ludicrous scripts.
In *Strait-Jacket,* she portrays a deranged woman who discovers her husband in bed with his lover and hacks their heads off.
After her release from a mental institution, she's suspected of a fresh series of beheadings.

Crawford caused the most damage to her reputation by accepting ludicrous scripts,
Tawdry grade-B entries churned out for quick profit.
After her release from a mental institution, she's suspected of a fresh series of beheadings.
The killer is revealed as Crawford's daughter.

In *Berserk!,* another bloodbath churned out for quick profit,
Crawford plays a ringmistress whose circus is plagued by a rash of gruesome murders.
The killer is revealed as Crawford's daughter.
Sadly, her last Hollywood film was the dismal *Trog.*

Crawford plays a ringmistress whose circus is plagued by a rash of gruesome murders.
She admitted these movies were terrible: "I made them because I needed the money or because I was bored or both."
Sadly, her last Hollywood film was the dismal *Trog,*
The most embarrassing enterprise to which she had ever subjected herself.

"I made them because I needed the money or because I was bored or both."
Unlike Crawford, Davis made repeated attempts to escape the low-budget horror mold,
Embarrassing enterprises to which she kept subjecting herself.
None were as stylish or suspenseful as *What Ever Happened to Baby Jane?*

Davis made repeated attempts to escape the low-budget horror mold.
As the sixties wore on, the films she was offered became more and more exploitive.
None were as stylish or suspenseful as *What Ever Happened to Baby Jane?*
She campaigned vigorously for the role of Martha in the movie version of *Who's Afraid of Virginia Woolf?*

As the sixties wore on, the films she was offered became more and more exploitive.
One of the biggest disappointments of her career was not getting the role
She'd campaigned vigorously for, Martha in the movie version of *Who's Afraid of Virginia Woolf?*
Instead, she ended up in *The Anniversary*, as the fiendish eye-patched mother of three sons, one of whom "likes to wear ladies' underthings."

It was one of the biggest disappointments of her career.
She cried when she saw herself in rushes.
She'd ended up in *The Anniversary*, as the fiendish eye-patched mother of three sons, one of whom "likes to wear ladies' underthings."
She's loud, over-the-top, unhinged, dangerous, and luminous.

Davis cried when she saw herself in rushes.
She slouches around in a fright wig, bedroom slippers, and makeup that looks put on with a putty knife.
She's loud, over-the-top, unhinged, dangerous, and luminous.
What Ever Happened to Baby Jane? is an excellent movie and well worth owning on DVD.

All This, and Heaven Too

[*The Films of Bette Davis*]

The Bride Came C.O.D., Payment on Demand.
The Letter Marked "Woman Dangerous, June Bride,
Cabin in the Cotton, Bordertown, Way Back Home."

What Ever Happened to Baby Jane? Housewife.
Winter Meeting: Satan Met a Lady, The Girl From
Tenth Avenue Hell's House, Bunny O'Hare.

That Certain Woman: Bad Sister (The Dark Horse),
The Old Maid (The Empty Canvas), The Nanny
(The Scapegoat), Wicked Stepmother (The Menace).

Now, Voyager, Parachute Jumper, Watch on the Rhine:
Fog Over Frisco (Storm Center), The Whales of August,
Waterloo Bridge. The Big Shakedown — So Big.

All About Eve — Ex-Lady, Jezebel. Three on a Match:
Kid Galahad, Jimmy the Gent, Special Agent Juarez.
The Rich Are Always With Us: Front Page Woman,

The Star, Hollywood Canteen. The Private Lives of
Elizabeth (The Virgin Queen) and Essex (The Man Who
Played God). Hush . . . Hush, Sweet Charlotte, It's Love

I'm After. Deception. The Great Lie. Another Man's
Poison Seed — Death on the Nile. 20,000 Years in Sing
Sing. Phone Call From a Stranger — Dead Ringer.

Bureau of Missing Persons: John Paul Jones, The
Working Man; Mr. Skeffington, The Man Who Came
to Dinner (The Catered Affair) — The Anniversary.

The Golden Arrow Skyward. Dark Victory In This Our
Life Of Human Bondage. A Stolen Life. Old Acquaintance:
The Scientific Cardplayer. Fashions of 1934. The Sisters'

Connecting Rooms. Beyond the Forest, The Petrified Forest,
The Corn Is Green. Pocketful of Miracles. Burnt Offerings.
Watcher in the Woods, Thank Your Lucky Stars The Little

Foxes Return From Witch Mountain, Where Love Has Gone.

Crack of old ice
 under new snow

The moon has come back
 into my poems

Watching the Late Movie with My Mother

It was our special time:
just the two of us
alone in the family room
on a Saturday night,
everybody else—my father, brother
and two younger sisters—
asleep in the back of the house.
She reclined on the brown couch;
I was sprawled on the carpet
in front of the TV, totally
absorbed in the drama
on the small screen:

Elizabeth Taylor in a white slip,
Paul Newman on crutches,
arguing in an upstairs bedroom;
Natalie Wood and Carolyn Jones sneaking
off from their summer camp
and canoeing, by moonlight,
to the adult resort across the lake;
or Tippi Hedren tiptoeing away
from her boss's safe, her
beige pump slowly slipping
out of her coat pocket.

My mother lay there
in her lavender bathrobe,
head propped on a couple of throw
pillows, with her double chin
and her salt-and-pepper hair,
bags under her eyes,
easily moved to tears
by love or death scenes.

During a used car
commercial, I fixed popcorn
in the kitchen, poured it
into the large green Tupperware

bowl, quickly added
melted butter and salt
as not to miss a minute
of the movie. I scooped
a small bowl for my mother,
grabbed napkins, set a glass
of ice water on a cork coaster
on the table next to the couch.

Often, she fell asleep
before the end and I'd have
to nudge her: "The movie's
over, Mom, go to bed."
Once alone, I quietly unlocked
the kitchen door and snuck
outside, my cigarettes tucked
in the pocket of my plaid robe.
In the driveway, I smoked
several in a row, ducking behind
a hedge whenever a car
came by, its headlights sweeping
the dark street.

Occasionally, a dog barked
on another block. Dew
shimmered on the dichondra
in our front yard. I looked up
at the moon, the trees, what
stars I could see through
the glow of the city in the
distance. I inhaled the last drags
deeply, doused the butt in curb water.
Then, as frightened and excited
as Marjorie Morningstar
or Marnie, I tiptoed back
into the house.

Written with a Pencil Found in Lorine Niedecker's Front Yard

Bewitched
     the boys were out
          in force

Drunken-
     ness and lust

—and full moon
bouncing back
          and forth that
black

above the bars

*

Last night
     it burned
          cigarette

tip
     thru old
          blanket

hole-punched
     gray paper
          sky

Tonight it
     outright
          blinded

One headlight
     or drive-in sci-fi
          eye

*

I've been
        alone
long enough

Even the moon
wears a ring

and is full

Ode to Thelma Ritter

There's no one like you in the movies
anymore, Thelma, no lovable, middle-aged
character actress, gravelly voiced and
hard-boiled, with a sharp-tongued flair
for the cynical as well as the comical. You
could work miracles with a little screen time,
turning out indelible performances in a matter
of minutes: Bette Davis's acerbic sidekick
in *All About Eve*, Jimmy Stewart's down-to-
earth nurse in *Rear Window*, Doris Day's
perpetually hung-over maid in *Pillow Talk*.
You played women with names like Clancy,
Aggie, Bertha, Birdie, Lottie, Leena, Della,
Stella, Sophie, Sadie, Maude, Mae, and Moe.
But what of you, Thelma? Online I find only
this mini-biography. Born in Brooklyn on
Valentine's Day in 1905. Trained at American
Academy of Dramatic Arts. Stage career
mostly unsuccessful. Married Joseph Moran
in 1927; briefly gave up acting to raise two
children. Started working again in radio in
1940. Bit part in *Miracle on 34th Street* launched
noteworthy screen career. Appeared in thirty
films between 1947 and 1968. Died of a heart
attack in 1969 in New York. Thelma, six times
you were nominated for Best Supporting
Actress, and six times you lost. You, who
could save any movie with your wisecracks!
A Google search uncovers this little-known fact:
"Shirley Booth was not the first choice to play
Hazel. Thelma Ritter was. Miss Ritter wanted
the role badly, but due to illness had to bow out."
Booth would win two Emmys in the early '60s
for playing television's sassiest maid — your
rightful part. O elusive trophies! O tired heart!
You, who survived the Titanic in one picture,
would say sadly, world-wearily, in the next:
"I have to go on making a living so I can die."

To Arielle and the Moon

The night reduced to a siren, a sigh:

Beautiful boy on the treadmill

Glimpsed sweating through sweating glass —

My new moon.

Sylvia's moon: a smiling skull

Snagged in witchy branches; fossil

Brushed free of blackest earth.

My last moon: an orange ball at rest, for an instant,

On the grey lake.

Wish list: dining set and dresser,

Boombox, thin black tie, boy-

Friend à la Madonna's "True Blue"

La la la la la la la

Your moon (tonight): a clouded X-ray.

I stand at a corner and stare up,

Both of us astonished

By its own secret light.

Who's There?

Iris or Olaf?
Captain Howdy?
Ephraim? Sybil's Pan?
The planchette rose off
the Ouija board and
floated midair.
Medea (the daughter)
screamed. Or did I
scream in my
seat, ten years old,
at that Saturday
matinee in Reseda?
Surely I did.
I *was* Medea.

A Poem Under the Influence

[for Jeffery Conway]

Last night I dreamt of Barbie, or to be precise, a Barbie outfit: a big pink gown
that came with unusual shoes: clear plastic half shells, about the size of her
    "Plantation Belle"
hat, sprinkled with silver glitter. Her feet fit into high-heel-shaped indentations
in the base of each shell. That's all I recall. I rarely remember my dreams.
It's July 22, two days after my birthday. Three months ago I wrote in my red
    journal:
From a dream: The ending of a short, uncollected poem by Anne Sexton:

"I drank my coffee
and contemplated the white candle."

The next day I wrote: *Dream: Feet half over the curb, Barry holds me by the back*
of my neck w/one hand, leans me forward. "What do you know about the
    Goddess, he asks.
"That she's powerful," I say, "And that I'm afraid of her." Between these two
    entries:
Why do I find rape scenes exciting? Further back, in January, I dreamt I was
    pissing blood
that looked like ketchup. This is more dream remembering than usual. Years
    pass,
it seems, and . . . nada. (A psychic once told me that means I do a lot of work
in the sleep state.) Though I tend to remember dreams during times of crisis or
    change.
In the summer of 1988, for instance, when I drove from Los Angeles to New
    York,
I remembered them like mad. That was a trip! Janet Gray and I tooling across
this great land of ours, chain smoking and reading out loud from the baroque
    second novel
of a "flamboyant" L.A. poet (a narcissist of pathological proportions), laughing
ourselves to tears. We stopped at McDonald's on a daily basis and ordered as
    healthily as possible
(in my case, a Quarter-Pounder with Cheese and carton of milk). Toward the
    beginning
of our journey (New Mexico, I think) one of Janet's dogs, a sweet Irish setter
    named Britt,

freaked out and had (we later figured) a stroke. She lay panting in the back
seat. Unrelenting August heat, no A/C. At one point I turned around and
     realized
Britt had died. Telling Janet, who was at the wheel, her cigarette smoke
     streaming
out the open window, was no easy thing. We must have been in Texas by then.

I am typing this on pink paper in tribute to Sylvia Plath, who wrote her great
     poems
on "pink, stiff, lovely-textured" Smith College stationery, her vision "special,
     rose-cast."
She even bought a pink light bulb for the room in which she worked. ("Life is
     all about
lighting," says Stevie Nicks—and she should know!) Also in tribute to
     Jacqueline Susann,
who pecked away on a hot pink Royal manual, and wrote (she said) subsequent
     drafts
of her novels on different-colored paper: pink, green, yellow, blue, white.
("She doesn't write," Gore Vidal said famously, "she types." Another critic
     jealous
of her huge success said she typed on a cash register.) Susann used (she said)
a blackboard and color-coordinated chalks (pink, green, yellow, blue, white) to
     chart
the progress of her characters and her plots. As a teenager I loved the idea of
     writing
being color-coordinated, like women's fashion accessories. Pink, green, yellow,
     blue, white—
the bright colors of Jackie's Pucci outfits, her kaleidoscopic "banana-split night-
     mares,"
which she liked because they were light and easy to wash on the road.
(New York, 1997: Ira and I shop for Pucci ties to wear to "The Other Jackie,"
a panel discussion "of the enduring influence of Jacqueline Susann," at The
     New School,
where I teach. Ira, who as editor-in-chief of Grove Press has brought *Valley of
     the Dolls*
back into print, moderates. I sit on stage with Jackie's friends, editors, and
     biographer,
Rex Reed among them. My tie—a cascade of gold, salmon, magenta, lime
     green, red-orange,

and pale pink tendrils and swirls—is my badge of honor. A slide of Jackie is
    projected
on a screen behind me as I stand at the podium and deliver my talk. I feel her
smiling down on me—Our Lady of "Literary Trash," who called inspiration
    "juice.")

Confession: I have in my possession two check stubs, one yellow and one pink,
of royalty payments for *Valley of the Dolls*, which I stole when, for ten days in
    the summer of 1998,
I cataloged Jackie's papers, photographs, and memorabilia. I'd been hired by
    the Susann estate and brought
out to Los Angeles—the only time I've flown first class. Kim Rosenfield and
    Rob
Fitterman were on that flight; we chatted in a waiting area at JFK. I was both
    elated and embarrassed
when first-class passengers were invited to board before the others, the pitiful
    commoners
who would have to crouch together in coach. "All poets should fly first class!"
I pronounced with mock egalitarianism. And in that vain rush forgot my
    laptop.
I was buckled in, blithely testing the legroom, before it dawned on me I'd left it
    behind.
Felt a fool as I dashed off the plane, past Kim and Rob, boarding by then, to
    retrieve it.
One of the first things the Susann executrix asked me to do was destroy all of
    Jackie's financial records.
"No one needs to see this," she insisted. I tried to convince her that the income
of "one of the best-selling novelists of all time" might be of interest to
    someone . . .
to no avail. I complied, but secretly plucked, at the last minute, five check
    stubs
from the trash. A forgivable theft, n'est-ce pas? I presented one to Ira (for luck),
one to Lynn Crosbie (for her unmatched—except maybe by me—devotion to
    J.S.),
one to Wayne Koestenbaum (for teaching *Valley* in his Pornographic
    Imagination class at The Graduate Center),
and kept two for myself. The pink stub is from Bernard Geis Associates for
"royalties on net sales of VALLEY OF THE DOLLS for the month of April
    1966."

Seated at a dining table piled with Jackie's scrapbooks, letters, and manuscripts,
it was impossible not to feel like a beggar at a banquet. Naively, I asked the
    executrix if there
were any extra *Love Machine* ankhs. She scoffed, said she'd just given one to
    Michele Lee, who would wear
it when she played Jackie in *Scandalous Me,* a terrible (is there any other kind?)
    made-for-TV movie.
Her response effectively put me in my place, and let me know that ankhs don't
    grow on trees,
at least not in the San Fernando Valley, where at fourteen I discovered *V.O.D.*
    in a paperback rack
in a Thrifty Drug Store, and where at forty-five I sifted through the remnants of
    Jackie's career.
Remnants haphazardly stuffed in a dozen or so boxes, collecting dust in an
    Encino garage.
How many popular authors have met such a fate? It was an honor, really, to get
    that close
to what was left of her life. The executrix did allow me to take a few keepsakes:
a poster, some duplicate photos, a manuscript page with Jackie's scribblings, an
    author copy of the French
edition of *La Vallée des Poupées: Vive comme l'éclair, Neely plongea dans un des*
    W.C. dont elle verrouilla la porte.
On entendit un bruit de chasse d'eau. Translated: Quick as lightning, Neely
    plunged into one
of the water closets whereupon she bolted the door. They heard the sound of a
    flush.

A couple nights ago I noticed, at the corner of Belmont and Clark, a clothing
    store called Pink Frog.
A few doors down, in the window of Hollywood Mirror: a vintage metal waste-
    basket, pale pink,
with painted seahorse, seaweed and starfish, and glued-on plastic pearls; and a
    pink feather boa.
On Clark: pink neon. On Buckingham: pink flowerbeds. On the train going
    down to Boy's Town:
a golden pinkishness, as of a rose's brief peak: sunset through a slit in distant
    storm clouds.
A steady stream of airplanes, in flight pattern over Andersonville, descending
    toward O'Hare.

Once, traveling from Los Angeles to New York, Ira upgraded us to business class
and we sat across the aisle from Eileen Heckart. I was certain the plane
     wouldn't crash
(my fear of flying was at fever pitch) because an Oscar winner was on board.
Once, Sharon Mesmer and I flew from New York to Baton Rouge; Andrei
     Codrescu
had invited us to read at LSU. We were assigned different rows. I had an aisle
     seat.
The man to my right, who worked on the crew of "Roseanne," didn't believe
     me
when I said I'd never seen the show. (I had no TV till 1990, when Ira and I
moved in together.) I tried to read but couldn't concentrate: an overweight
woman had left first class and stood yakking with passengers in coach. She kept
bumping me. It was, of course, Ms. Roseanne Barr. I refused to look up from
     my book.
Once, Ricki Lake graciously let me go ahead of her while boarding a flight.
Once, Jack Skelley and I drank scotch flying cross-country; I'd brought a fifth of
     J & B in my bag.
October, 1982: I was finally going to New York City. How excited and
     frightened I was.
Tim Dlugos and Dennis Cooper (he'd flown out earlier than me and Jack) met
     us at JFK.
My first glimpse of Manhattan, through the window of our cab: the skyline—
so majestic and arresting—rising silently, at twilight, above the traffic and noise.
That sparkling panorama would always, during the years I'd later live there,
     returning tired
or weary from some journey, bring the magic back. Except at the end,
     naturally, after 9/11.
I stayed with Tim—host extraordinaire—in Brooklyn: Cobble Hill: his
     apartment on Strong Place
and for fourteen days ran around the Big Apple as if it were Disneyland. At an
     opening
I met Joe Brainard. I remember standing with him, both of us awkward and
     shy,
and glimpsing, through the crowd, Martha Diamond's blazing skyscrapers. Late
one night Eileen Myles and I rode the Staten Island Ferry—just like in her
     poem
"Romantic Pain" (we both caught colds). I visited Ted Berrigan and Alice
     Notley

on St. Mark's Place. Ted, "huge of frame," bedridden in the middle of their
     railroad flat,
cigarette ash dusting his beard and clothes, asked me to go buy him some Pepsi;
I was happy to comply. "For David, Civilized Poet and graceful guest, all the
     best,"
he wrote in one of the books I had him sign. He knew I was there for Alice:
     "See,"
he called out to her, "I told you someday they'd come to see *you*." (In time I'd
     fall
in love with his work as well.) Alice and I sat in the front room and shared a
     six-pack
of Budweiser (the tall cans). "Delirious afternoon," she wrote in one of her
     books.
And in another: "Oh God he wrote all over his—Am I this failure a Woman?
     Save me".
Tom Carey had arranged for me to meet James Schuyler at the Chelsea Hotel.
Running behind (drinks with Cheri Fein), I called to say I'd be late. Tom
     consulted
Schuyler and came back to the phone: "Jimmy says not to bother to come."
     Stunned,
I stammered, "Well, tell him I think he's the best living American poet." The
     next morning,
Tim shook me awake. Tom had called. When he told Schuyler what I'd said,
     Schuyler snapped,
"You can tell the little idiot he just missed meeting the best living American
     poet."
I moaned, prone on the fold-out couch. (Later, thankfully, Jimmy and I
     became
friends.) Tim loomed: "You drink too much." If you spot it you got it, as they
     say.
Soon both of us would pass through the Looking-Glass, into our sober lives.
Once, Ira and I had breakfast in Paris, lunch in London, and dinner in New
     York—in one day.
I didn't know such a thing was possible. Once, Dennis, Ira, and I went on every
ride in Fantasyland (something I'd always wanted to do as a child): Alice's
descent, Mr. Toad's Wild Ride, Peter Pan's flight over London at night—all
     those
tiny lights! The Magic Kingdom was ours: no lines. *Of such moments is
     happiness made.*

The next pink thing I see I'm going to put in this poem. "That guy needs more
   air in his tires."
"I don't think I know how to have fun." "We should have taken Lake Shore
   Drive."
Seven days before Christmas, Bob and I are stuck in traffic on 90/94, Dan Ryan
   Expressway,
downtown Chicago. We're driving to Cleveland, in Bob's black TrailBlazer, to
   see
the exhibition of Supremes gowns at the Rock and Roll Hall of Fame. "My
   camera
sounds sick." "We've been on the road an hour and we're not out of Chicago
   yet."
Fred (our nickname for Bob's Magellan GPS [Global Positioning System]) is
   our guide.
He continually interrupted me ("slight right turn in .5 miles"; "remain on the
   current road")
when I read Bob the beginning of the poem. This is a straight stretch, so Fred's
   finally quiet.
"I think we're in Indiana." Krazy Kaplans Costume Castle. "I hate having
   dandruff."
"I hadn't noticed." Rest area: we both pee. Bob's first glimpse of Manhattan
   was from New Jersey,
driving in from Philadelphia. He fell for the city right out of the Holland
   Tunnel—
the starkness of Canal Street at night; businesses with rolled-down gates, all
   locked up and
guarded; the aggressiveness of the driving a great rush. Eventually he'd
   convince
his boss to transfer him East. "I love all these lines and then all these cylinders
   out here."
"Let's talk about Scott again." "No, let's talk about Rafael." Amish Acres. "Oh,
there's snow." "According to Fred we have four hours and four minutes to go."
God bless America: an endlessly repeating background—like on *The
   Flintstones*—of the same
fast-food restaurants and large chains: McDonald's, Wal-Mart, Dairy Queen,
   Dunkin'
Donuts, Wendy's, Linens 'n Things, Home Depot, Burger King, Super Target,
   Taco

Bell, KFC. After a nap, I slip in a Supremes CD. *Though the love I give is not returned*
for that boy my heart still yearns. "I suppose The Supremes' lyrics were not the best guide to life."
"I mean occasionally I'd have sloppy, desperate, drunken sex." "Look at that windmill."
Crooked Creek. The Candy Cane Christmas Shoppe (open year round). "A little man-made lake
with some houses around it." "I wouldn't want to live there—this or any other life." Breast
cancer ribbon bumper sticker (the next pink thing). Welcome to Ohio. Pretty cemetery.

Over the years,
many of the gowns
worn by The Supremes
were given descriptive
names by the group
and their fans. For
ease of identification,
all the gowns in this
exhibit are titled.

Black Swirls
White De Mink
Purple Fantasy
Turquoise Freeze
Pink Feathers
Crème de Menthe
Carousel
Yellow Wool
Tropical Lilac
Black Diamonds
Pink Lollipops
Feathered Bronze
Goldie
Black Butterfly
Green Valley Fringe
Cotton Candy

Blue Icicles
Orange Freeze
Green Petals
Red Hot
Sunburst

There was even a dress called Sophisticated Lady, like Barbie's biggest and
    pinkest
outfit from the mid-sixties: *Romantic old rose taffeta ball gown with silver filigree
    lace*
*trim on bodice and drape of skirt. Silver tiara, long white gloves, pink pearls and
    evening slippers.*
*Fitted American Beauty Rose velveteen evening coat, lined to match gown, has
    dainty silver buttons.*
This was Barbie's most expensive ensemble at the time: $5.00. Her wedding
    set, Bride's Dream,
cost $3.50; the doll itself (with red jersey swimsuit, pearl earrings, shoes, and
"special wire stand to keep Barbie on her feet for all Fashion Shows") cost
    $3.00.
Confession: I recently purchased Sophisticated Lady from a Barbie dealer for
    $150.00—
"NM/C" (near mint/complete); "Crisp gown with glitter version tiara" (Mattel
produced the outfit with two kinds of headbands: clear plastic with molded-in
    silver glitter
and solid gray plastic with no glitter; I'm sure most Barbie collectors prefer the
    former)
—one of several Christmas presents to myself. Confession: this is not the first
    time
I've purchased Sophisticated Lady. My collecting: a saga I doubt I'll ever fully
    understand.
Let's just say that—like many collectors—I've bought and purged, only to buy
    again.
Confession: last Monday (February 21) at Columbia College, I gave my poetry
    workshop
a writing assignment (Joe's I Remember) and went to my office to bid on Bride's
    Dream
on eBay. A gorgeous example, NRFB (never removed from box). I got it for
    $430.00
(a decent price), placing my bid nine seconds before the end of the auction.

How the heart races, bid sniping on eBay, waiting until seconds before the
        auction closes
to click "Confirm Bid." Confession: this is not the first time I've purchased
        Bride's Dream—
loose or NRFB. It's ironic, I said to my therapist, that at this particular moment
(over Ira/ready and willing to date/feeling like there's room for a relationship in
        my life)
I should find myself buying (again) Barbie's wedding dress. I did, after all, sell
the previous NRFB Bride's Dream I owned on eBay right after Ira and I broke
        up.
"I wouldn't mind having a wedding ring," I said to Bob not too long ago, idly
        twisting
a flattened straw wrapper around my ring finger. "You might want to find a
        boyfriend
first," he said drolly. Ira always wanted rings; I resisted. Instead, we bought
St. Christopher medals at Tiffany's. Had them engraved with each other's
        name
and wrapped, with white ribbon, in little boxes—my first taste of Tiffany blue.
December, 1992. One of the most romantic gifts: it's what the narrator of
        Breakfast at Tiffany's
gives Holly Golightly as a Christmas present. For years I wouldn't get on an
        airplane without
that St. Christopher around my neck. *Holly was not a girl who could keep
        anything, and surely by now*
she has lost that medal, left it in a suitcase or some hotel drawer. Unlike Holly,
        I've held onto mine.

What a stroke of pink luck that *What a Way to Go!* should come out on DVD
        while I am writing
this. A movie I first saw the year it was released (1964) and which had a
        monumental effect
on my young mind. How to capture that sense of rapture? I'm eleven. I'm
        sitting with
a group of neighborhood boys at the Northridge Theater, down in front,
        beneath that massive
Cinemascope screen. A couple of our mothers sit a few rows back. Shirley
        MacLaine
(wearing a black bikini) walks into a completely pink universe: pink swimming
        pool, pink

patio furniture, pink Grecian statues, pink plants and trees. In the next scene, MacLaine emerges

from a pink limousine wearing nothing but pink: pink slinky gown, pink floor-length mink,

pink earrings, purse, shoes, gloves. Most astonishing of all: her towering pink wig. I've written

about this elsewhere: upswept "swirls of cotton-candy-like pink hair." Pity, if you will, this

budding homosexual, this strange child ensconced in the dark in the suburbs of Los Angeles

the year after JFK was assassinated, transfixed by such pinkness. Did he share his pink epiphany

with the other boys? with his mother? Or did he secret it away, let it dominate his overactive

imagination like so many of his interests—Barbie paramount among them—unacceptable in

a boy. I remember that *What a Way to Go!* was on a double bill with *That Man From Rio*,

but don't remember how (or if) I responded to Jean-Paul Belmondo's homely good looks.

The Beatles (already a sensation: "I Want to Hold Your Hand" topped the *Billboard* charts in

February '64) would soon clue me in: contrary to popular sentiment, I thought Ringo was

the sexy one. Later: Sonny Bono and Bekim Fehmiu (of *The Adventurers*) turned me on.

I believe I saw a photograph of the latter wearing a skimpy black bathing suit, in a magazine.

What would I have done without *Playboy's* "History of Sex in the Cinema" pictorials?

And one in particular: July, 1968. I turned fifteen that summer, was masturbating

furtively, whenever I could. There was a photo in the spread that I couldn't get enough of:

two guys, one blond and one dark, naked except for fig leafs covering their genitals,

talking to a naked woman (who resembled Natalie Wood). The way the darkly handsome

man looks down at the woman—intently, licentiously—drove me wild. As did
　　the fact that

his fig leaf fails to cover, completely, the pouch that holds his crotch. As did
　　the idea

that whatever he wanted to do to the woman would involve the more feminine
　　blond man.

A few pages later: a rape scene from a sword and sandal epic: two soldiers
　　pinning

a maiden down—its attraction always confusing. Next to it: Keir Dullea and
　　Rossana Podestà

embracing, wet and naked. Dullea's expression undid me: half-closed eyes and
　　parted lips:

ecstatically surrendered to desire, as if stoned. I've been haunted by his beauty
　　ever since.

Did I mention the pink plastic DVD case? An all-pink Shirley MacLaine
　　adorns

both the cover and the DVD. The whole pink package designed by some
　　queen, no doubt.

Was it obvious I was looking at, rather than recalling from memory, that
　　Playboy pictorial?

In our travels, Ira and I scoured flea markets and antique malls: he for modern
　　furniture

and retro household items, I for bits and pieces of the past. I picked up a few
　　copies

of the slick men's magazine along the way. (Its centerfolds—what most boys
　　couldn't wait

to open wide—still terrify to some extent.) And picked up all manner of movie
　　memorabilia,

including stills, lobby cards, and posters from *What a Way to Go!* Why
　　shouldn't I try

to possess that pink world? Or each miniature piece of Barbie's vast, highly
　　accessorized

universe? Or every Yardley Slicker I can win on eBay? *Pocketa-pocketa.*
　　(Attachment, as I

once discussed with Ann Lauterbach, is a powerful thing. We were walking
　　across

Rutgers campus at sunset, on the way to her reading. The sky was shot with
　　streaks

of hot, almost phosphorescent pink. When we stopped to admire it, I said:
    "Nature's
really putting on a show for us.") And why shouldn't I also extol the dark side of
    attachment,
to all that horrified or traumatized? Like movies that scared the hell out of me
when I was a child. The first—I don't know the title—involved an underwater
    death.
A fifties black-and-white sci-fi flick? Futuristic submarines? A man tries to
    swim
through a circular passageway, but it contracts, closes and traps him, and he
    drowns.
I remember the horror of it, how I gasped in identification, couldn't breathe.
    My parents
were out for the evening. Mrs. Snyder, from around the block, was babysitting.
She used to let us stay up later than usual and watch movies on TV; we'd make
root beer floats and Jiffy Pop. In fact, the contracting circular passageway in the
    movie
resembled a flat silver Jiffy Pop pan, how it pinwheels toward the center. Are
my memories commingling? Then came *Invaders from Mars*, with its eerie
    music
and the sandpit behind the little boy's house that kept swallowing the towns-
    people:
they returned zombie-like, a strange implant in the base of their necks. I saw it
    at a revival house
in San Francisco in the mid-seventies and was surprised by how silly it was; it
    had
haunted me so. The murder raid in *The Searchers* also stayed with me: a
    pioneer family
massacred by marauding Comanches. I watched it two or three times in a row
    one Saturday
at my friend Mark's house, on his portable black-and-white TV. "Million
    Dollar Movie": Channel 9
would run the same film all weekend—an obsessive's dream in those pre-VHS
    days. Was amazed
years later to discover that Lucy, one of the daughters captured by the Indians, is
    murdered
offscreen. I could have sworn there was such a scene, so vividly had I imagined
    it. Was also
amazed to learn that *The Searchers* is in color: it had for so long been black-
    and-white in my mind.

———

Then came *Queen of Outer Space:* beneath her elaborate mask (gold, glittery,
     with swirly antennae) hideous pink,
red, and black radiation burns. Then *The Hypnotic Eye:* beautiful women, in a
     trance,
disfigure themselves: one, shampooing her hair at her kitchen stove, sets herself
     on fire;
another washes her face with acid. Then *Bluebeard's Ten Honeymoons:* George
Sanders disposing of a woman's body on a dark train track, burning other
     victims
in his fireplace—the telltale smoke billowing from his chimney late at night.
Then *Blackbeard, the Pirate:* buried up to his neck on a beach, he drowns as the
     tide comes in.
Other indelible scenes from a childhood spent watching, on TV and at
     matinees, as many movies as possible:
Tom and Becky Thatcher lost in the caves in *The Adventures of Tom Sawyer;* a
     woman stoned to death
in *Barabbas,* Anthony Quinn condemned to the sulfur mines in the same
     movie; Ben-Hur's mother and sister
cowering in the shadows of a leaf-littered courtyard, lepers in rags; Brandon De
     Wilde rescuing
Carol Lynley from the abortionist at the end of *Blue Denim;* Inger Stevens and
     Don Murray shot
(not really, it turns out) at the end of *The Borgia Stick;* the woman's disembod-
     ied talking head
in *The Brain That Wouldn't Die;* the pilot bisected by an airplane propeller in
     Catch-22;
Lee Remick harassed by a psychopath in *Experiment in Terror;* a blood-splat-
     tered kitchen in
The House on Greenapple Road; a skeleton prodding Vincent Price's wife into a
     vat of acid
in *House on Haunted Hill;* the river raft caught in the rapids in *How the West
     Was Won* (it breaks
apart, Agnes Moorehead drowns); a dead body in a car trunk in *The Lady in the
     Car with*
Glasses and a Gun; a mother and child engulfed in molten lava in *The Last
     Days of Pompeii;*
the rape in *Last Summer;* Dorothy Malone trapped on a sinking ship in *The
     Last Voyage,*

Robert Stack frantically trying to free her; the cruelty (to Shirley Temple) of
    Miss Minchin
in *The Little Princess*; Jill St. John attacked by man-eating vines, a native girl
    chased
through a giant spider web tunnel in *The Lost World*; the rape in *Rider on the
    Rain*;
Rock Hudson gagged and screaming, being wheeled to extinction at the end of
    Seconds;
the dismemberment of Sebastian Venable in *Suddenly, Last Summer*; the
    haunted house
in *13 Ghosts*; Rod Taylor saving Yvette Mimieux from drowning and from the
    hairy,
blue-skinned, subterranean mutants in *The Time Machine*; Diana Barrymore
    (Dorothy
Malone) self-destructing in *Too Much, Too Soon*; the deaths — by runaway
    wagon,
by Indians, by flash flood — in *Westward the Women*; Irene Papas murdered by
    angry villagers
in *Zorba the Greek*. In one movie, or maybe it was a TV show, a stewardess
    sucked out
of an airplane. How ill the thought of such a fate made me feel. It felt real.
    Still,
I had a desperate desire to see, to know about murder and death and
    destruction.
I begged my mother to let me watch *Children of the Damned* (kids with
    telepathic powers
and glowing eyes!), but she refused. Why she let me see *The Nanny*, with
    demented,
murderous Bette Davis, is a mystery; she must have thought it was a sweet little
    story about
a children's nurse. The few times my father took me to the movies, it was to
    epics like
Lawrence of Arabia and *Cleopatra*. Both bored me to tears. Too young to
    appreciate
Liz's bad acting and heavy makeup, I sat waiting, waiting for her to be bitten by
    the asp.

———

Another day (July 9), another piece of pink paper. I'd wanted, when I started
    this poem,
to write it rapidly: twenty stanzas in as many days. Here it is a year later, and
I'm not even halfway done. So my early fifties whiz by. A few years are all we
    have—
yet there is a sense of timelessness in the temporal. One gets lost in dailiness,
    in one's own
compulsions, in the never-ending to-do list. In my case: the Post-its (pink,
    green, yellow, blue)
that for over twenty years (since I got sober) have reminded me to pay my rent,
to take out the trash, to call or write someone back. And have caught the
    fleeting image
or thought, things (especially this past year) to include in poems. "Pink Poets,"
    for instance.
A preliminary list: Sexton and Plath, James Schuyler, William Carlos Williams,
    Elaine Equi.
Or "Scorpio Poets" (here we have some overlap): Sexton and Plath, Schuyler,
Alice Notley, Amy Gerstler—poets whose work has meant the world to me.
Maybe it's my Scorpio moon: all I have to do is touch one of their poems and I
    get ideas.
So many poets, so few kind ones (the aforementioned excluded). *Lawsamercy,*
    honeychil'!
What you spect? 'Taint like you was entering a nunnery or nutin', when you took
    up da pen.
Why, today, do I think of unkindness? She of the horse manure, murderer of
    woodchucks,
who after I wined and dined her the day of her reading, treated her like royalty
    really,
trashed my work in a condescending email. How that hurt—an abrupt,
    inexplicable attack.
Threw me for a loop early last summer; not till I started this poem did I begin
    to shake
her meanness off. Or he of the Paleolithic vulva, who so childishly lashed out
    when
I had the audacity to reject (rather tactfully, I thought) his "first-rate" (his words)
    poems.
To live to seventy or eighty, enjoying long and successful careers as professional
    poets,

and not to develop a sense of grace, let alone the simplest manners. What's
    wrong with
this picture? In the seventies, when I was studying with Ann Stanford at Cal
    State Northridge,
she returned from a trip to New York, where she'd given a poetry reading.
    When
I asked her how it went, she said, "I hate John Ashbery." It was the only unkind
    thing
I ever heard her say. I wish I'd asked her to explain. Mean poets? A concept,
    at that point,
I don't think I'd have wanted to accept. Poetry was akin to a religious calling.
    So naive.

Why dwell on the negative. Better to look pinkly through a glass at the
    tarnished past,
count my blessings (on both hands), and call it a day. But I have to ask: why,
    early on,
did Ann Stanford (my mentor) and Rachel Sherwood (my first poet friend) both
    say,
independent of each other, that they hated John Ashbery? A warning? Of
    course Rachel
was talking about his work. Well, many years later I would feel, at a party at
    Darragh Park's,
little J.A.'s sting. And having been stung, feel vindicated when I came across
    the following
in Ted Berrigan's *Train Ride:* "The grotesque John Ashbery of / the bad
    character".
Of course Ted is being tongue in cheek. In all fairness, Ashbery was pleasant
    enough
on other occasions: Jimmy's birthday dinners at Chelsea Central, the day
    Jimmy's ashes
were buried at Little Portion Friary. Douglas Crase once told me that, walking
    with Ashbery
in SoHo, he pointed out where Ira and I lived, said he'd recently been to one of
    our parties.
Ashbery looked up toward our apartment and snipped, *"I've* never been invited
to one of their parties." An anecdote as gratuitous as it is telling? I often felt,
at those glittering New York literary cocktail parties, like a Christian in the
    lions' den.

Once, when Ira and I arrived at an Upper West Side party for Wayne
    Koestenbaum,
the hostess (a Knopf poet with whom I'd been anthologized) barreled past us to
    greet an
obviously more important guest. She slammed into my shoulder, then gave me
    an angry look,
as if her foyer were a rush-hour subway. I still cringe whenever I happen upon
    her name.
Oh that was a black decade, the nineteen-nineties. First Tim died, then Jimmy,
then Joe; everyone scrambling, all the while, dog-eat-dog style, for the success,
    for the fabulous,
supercalifragilistic fame they felt entitled to. New York doesn't stop to grieve
the loss of poets, or of youthful idealism. One is left to tend one's own wounds
    in
one's SoHo loft, corner of West Broadway and Spring, as high rents force out
    the mom-and-pops
and the art galleries flee to Chelsea and one winds up living—a true prisoner of
    New York—
in the center of an outdoor upscale mall teeming with shop-till-you-drop tourists
    and daytrippers.
Ira tried, in his way, to protect me. But how many times, upon entering the
    lions' den,
did he leave me to fend for myself? He knew how to work a room; it was one of
    his gifts.
I both admired and resented him for it. "And you are?" Such vile condescen-
    sion from an
acquaintance, a real "vomit number" (to quote Truman Capote), at an Alice
    Notley reading at St. Mark's.
If I had it to do over again, I'd say "You know perfectly well who I am" and turn
my back. Regrettably I just stood there and listened to her boast her accom-
    plishments.
In January 1990, I read at Intuflo in SoHo—Broadway and Thompson. Little
    did I know
that, within a few months, I'd be living with Ira a block away. I read "Eighteen
    to
Twenty-One" that night, and couldn't understand why the audience thought my
    sex life
was so funny. Jill Hoffman came up to read after me and made a flippant
    remark

about my work. "Don't call David's poems dirty!" Eileen Myles yelled from the
    back
of the room. Eileen had balls—I loved her for that. Ironically, our seven-year
    friendship
would soon come to an end. Susan Wheeler was also at that reading. I nerv-
    ously asked her,
as I was being introduced, to hold my cigarettes. That was the beginning of a
    beautiful friendship.

Once, in a workshop, Ann Stanford told us never to use "pink" or "gossamer" in
    a poem.
She had a personal prejudice against these words. I agreed with her about
    "gossamer,"
but "pink"? I proceeded (youthful rebellion?) to pinken all of my poems.
To this day, if I can fit "pink" in a poem, I do. Just now, on Byron's morning
    walk,
we passed the woman who lives four doors down Hollywood Ave., Mrs. Broyle
(according to the plaque on her house). She was sitting in the swing on her
    front porch,
wearing a pink T-shirt. "How is your dog?" I asked. (A few weeks ago she'd told
    me
her fourteen-year-old Schnauzer, Micky, was having heart problems.) "I had to
put him down." "I'm sorry to hear that." "I miss him. We get attached to
    them, you know.
They're like children." She gave Byron three of Micky's treats: one bacon and
    two
green biscuits. Home, he still expected the usual post-walk treat, so I gave him
    half
a beef biscuit. Then he scarfed down his breakfast. Hard to believe Byron
    himself
is almost fourteen. Just now, while I was making toast, Peni called to tell me
    that she
and Jen (Maureen Seaton's daughter) were in an accident on the way to the
    airport
and are in transit to the hospital with arm injuries, that they might need me to
walk their dog Jane later this afternoon. Last night after a meeting, Peni and
    Jen
took me out to dinner for my birthday. I spilled Diet Coke on Jen's new white
    skirt.

"I'm so sorry, Jen." She almost burst into tears. Felt awful, blamed it on full
    moon,
Mercury retrograde madness. The past few days have been wild: no Internet
connection, Byron and I caught in downpour, cab driver from hell, therapy felt
like five minutes, restaurant full, slow service, no cake on birthday, mistakes,
delays, *Night of the Living Dead* shoppers coming at me with carts in the super-
    market.
Thought yesterday (Friday) was Saturday. Today (Saturday) is July 23, three
    days
after my birthday. I'd intended to write yesterday, July 22 (the day I started this
    poem
a year ago—full circle, perfect), but Priscilla called: Patrick was at St. Joseph's
with a burst appendix: she and Megan were going to see him, I should come
    with them.
Megan brought Patrick a stuffed dog; I bought him a pink feather boa in the
    hospital
gift shop. Patrick just out of surgery: his usual humorous self. His immediate
    impulse,
upon seeing us, was to crack a joke, but it hurt too much to laugh. Priscilla and
    I sat with him
as he faded in and out. He said he thought, when he first came to, that he was
    playing
"Frère Jacques" on his recorder. *Are you sleeping?* The association (he said)
    was obvious.

Last Wednesday (July 27) on Wabash Ave. I passed a guy in a pink shirt.
    "David?"
It was poet Larry Janowski. "Oh, hi." I was lost in post-therapy reverie (I'd
    cried, envisioning
wholeness) and fumbled the moment, kept walking, the opportunity for human
    contact
taking a back seat to interiority, and that flash of passing pink. The things I've
    missed
in life, lost in my own head. I don't know how many times I've learned (after
    the fact)
that people have felt I slighted them, when in actuality I simply wasn't present,
    fully,
but absorbed in my own (usually grim) imaginings. "I thought you were
    conceited."

"No, just cripplingly shy." Once, when a certain individual (a publisher of gay and

lesbian poetry) treated me rudely, I asked a mutual friend why he disliked me.

Friend later reported: "He says you snubbed him at an AA meeting five years ago."

Once, walking home from high school, Susan Dick (redheaded, freckled, bespectacled)

said, "David Trinidad, you have a black cloud over you." All too true. But Sue, how to

disperse it? I remember seeing, in a john at school, a sticker above a urinal: RAP LINE

and the number: the prefix plus R-A-P-P. I must have been sixteen or seventeen, had

already tried confession, but bolted (never to return to the Catholic church) when

the priest admonished, in an emphatic whisper: *You must put these evil thoughts out of your mind.*

I dialed (one night from a gas station phone booth) and a man named David answered.

Agonized, I somehow managed to give voice to my problem. Thank God David was on

the other end of the line. We became friends (I called him frequently from that phone booth);

in an attempt to help me, he took me to talk to a counselor at a free clinic. Scared

and confused, I sat across from this middle-aged woman and once again blurted

my secret: *I think I'm a homosexual. What should I do? How can I meet others like myself?*

Somewhere in the black depths of my memory is the image of her expression —

indignant? outraged? cruel?—as she uttered: "What do you think I am, a pimp?"

Thirty years later, I asked David (he himself had come out by then; we'd stayed in

touch) what he remembered of this event. Nothing, to my great disappointment.

I was in therapy with Laura in New York, casting back to the angry blanks of adolescence.

I hoped that David had complained about this woman to the clinic. I wanted to believe

she'd been chastised in some way. I remember, at eighteen, fingering my
    shoelace as I sat
across from Dr. Phelan. My parents sent me to him (to "change" me) after the
    rape.
"I can't change you," he said during our first session, "but I can help you
    become
a better-adjusted homosexual." The path had twisted, turned; I'd been dealt
    some pretty
rough blows, but somehow had ended up in his office. Under his guidance, I
    sat my parents
down and told them I was gay, that I intended to pursue the lifestyle of my
    choice.
My mother cried. "I take no responsibility for this," insisted my father. Since
    he
was paying for it, and since it had in his eyes failed, he cancelled my therapy.
 "I'm going to miss you, David," Dr. Phelan said, at the end of our final session.
How sad and special his words made me feel, lost as I was, leaving his office for
    the last time.

Pink Moonbeams: my most recent eBay acquisition: late sixties two-piece
    negligee set,
in soft or hot pink: gown topped by white lace bodice with pale pink ribbon
    straps
and flower detailing; peignoir lace-lined, with pink marabou sleeve trim. I got
    the hot
pink version. Bought it from dolldogfan, a seller I purchase from regularly.
    Her
real identity is Karen Caviale, one of the editors of *Barbie Bazaar*, "the official
    Barbie
doll collector's magazine." I remember reading, many years ago, an article in
    Barbie Bazaar
about a woman who collected "pink box"—not vintage, but the garish blonde
    dolls
Mattel produces to cash in on the collectors' market. She filled an entire room
with "pink box." Then one night lightning struck this room and her collection
went up in smoke. Poof—just like that. The great collector in the sky
    punishing
her for her gullibility, her poor taste? I love the idea of lightning hitting its pink
    mark.

But all of this is gratuitous, given where I am in my therapy and my poem.
"Do you want to talk about the rape?" Prem asked last Wednesday. "No,
I'd rather wait and see what comes out in the poem." But I did tell him my
    dream:
I was trying to escape from a large house (a mansion?), had just made it out the
front door when Nick (the man who raped me) popped out of a closet and tried
to drag me back in. Something was printed on his gray T-shirt—a word? He
    seemed
more powerful: had he developed super powers? Byron was somewhere in the
house, in danger. I was worried that Nick would hurt him. Dreamt this three
    and
a half weeks ago, on July 12, my first remembered dream in over eight months.
Dr. Phelan once said there were warning signs that I could have read, had I
    been more
aware, about Nick's character. Did I see and not see? I honestly didn't know. I
    was so
inexperienced. Eighteen, on my own for the first time (I'd gotten a job as a
    stock boy
at K-Mart, rented a guest house in Reseda), first year of college, living out a
    fantasy
of myself as a free spirit, like Holly Golightly ("*Traveling*") or Patty Duke in *Me,*
    Natalie.
Did the rape ever take the wind out of those pink sails. Nick: "Do you have any
    lubricant?"
What did I know about anal intercourse. So he fucked me dry, a steak knife
    (my
mother had given me a set when I moved out) in his right hand. I remember
    that
he whacked my thigh with it, drawing blood, when I resisted, to let me know he
meant business. I remember that, before he turned on me, I played him the
    soundtrack
to *Valley of the Dolls* and he said the theme song was about suicide, an
    interpretation
I didn't understand. I remember that I said to him: "I hope you find what
    you're looking for."
Something I'd heard in a movie? And that that was what made him turn.
    "What
do you mean by that?" Thank God my neighbor (a blonde woman who raised
    chinchillas)

saw us scuffle: Nick pulled me back into the guest house when I tried to leave. And that

she knew my last name: she looked up my parents in the white pages. Nick answered

the phone when it rang, held the receiver to my ear (he had tied my hands behind

my back). "Are you in trouble?" said my mother, "Do you need help? Just say yes or no."

"Yes." "*Put him on.*" "She wants to speak to you." Nick listened, hung up, untied me,

and left in a hurry. I later learned what she'd said to him: "David's father and I

will be there in a few minutes. We have a gun. If you're smart, you'll leave right now."

My parents did arrive within minutes, and my mother did have a loaded pistol

in her purse—like a woman in an Almodóvar film. My three-month stint as a

free spirit ended then and there. I went home, never to return to that guest house,

except to collect my things: a beaded curtain, some sheets I'd tie-dyed in high school,

posters of Janis Joplin and Jane Fonda, a framed photograph of Bette Davis that I'd bought

at an antique store on Ventura Blvd. I'd have been too afraid to continue living there anyway.

On my mantelpiece: a pink vinyl Barbie and Ken case, a pink painting by Denise Duhamel,

and a 24-inch-long pink plastic Remco Showboat. The case shows Ken in Tuxedo

and Barbie in Enchanted Evening, her famous pale pink satin gown, with its slim

skirt and long, draping train. I bought it last summer, when Joris and I braved the sales room

at the Barbie National Convention. I paid him to drive me to the Hyatt Regency O'Hare,

where I spent (quite quickly) the better part of a sizable tax return. Joris (who,

being an *X-Files* addict, was fascinated by the climate of frenzied collecting)

snapped a number of photographs: row upon row of dolls, impervious in their clear-lidded

coffins; bubblecuts with price tags tied like nooses around their necks; a bin filled
with doll heads ("$7 each")—a tangled, post-guillotine mass. When I was in Miami
last February, I admired Denise's paintings of Olive Oyl's boot-clad feet (which
hang in Maureen Seaton's guest apartment, where I was staying). "Would you paint
something pink for me?" I asked the night Denise, Maureen, Nick, and I ordered in
Chinese food and played Celebrity. In June Denise sent me "Milkshake," a pink drink
with glued-on doodads: green and pink straws, plastic musclemen figures, and felt flowers.
The Remco Showboat is one of three toy theaters I was obsessed with as a child.
It came with punch-out characters and scenery, and scripts for four plays: Pinocchio,
Cinderella, Wizard of Oz, and Heidi. Pull tab to lift curtain: Dorothy (holding Toto)
and the Witch of the West stand center stage. Behind them we see Dorothy's house.
Under it: a pair of feet wearing red-and-white-striped stockings. The shoes are gone.
Twisting into the distance: the tornado that transported her to this strange land.
Shirley Temple's Magnetic TV Theater (by Amsco) came with actors, props, and backdrops
for Goldilocks and the Three Bears, Red Riding Hood, and Sleeping Beauty. By grasping
a Figure Guide and placing your hand beneath the stage, directly below an actor
set in a Figure Base, you could make magnetic contact and move that actor forward,
backward, sideways, around in circles, and in and out the exits—like magic!
Somewhere there's a Kodak slide of me, age five, kneeling beside my Shirley
Temple theater. 1958, the year before Barbie was born: I wear a crewcut and a wistful smile.
The Barbie and Ken Little Theatre, which my sisters got for Christmas in 1964, haunted
my waking hours and rendered me sleepless at night. Tortured gay boy on the verge

of puberty. How could he be anything but gaga over the magnificently detailed costumes
Mattel designed for this sturdy, easy-to-assemble structure. Red Riding Hood
had a basket with checked napkin and wax rolls (to take to Grandma) and a gray plush
wolf head for Ken. Cinderella had a patched "poor" dress and broom, and—
after her transformation—a yellow satin ball gown with silver applique, lamé bodice,
and white tulle overskirt. The Prince had a green and gold brocade jacket with rhinestone
buttons, white lace collar and cuffs, green velvet cape, gold cap with white plume
and jewel, and a magenta velvet pillow for Barbie's glass (clear plastic) closed-toe pump.
At the National Barbie Convention in San Diego in 1997, I purchased Red Riding Hood
and the Wolf, NRFB, for $795.00. The following year, Ira and I flew to Las Vegas
to witness Damon and Naomi's marriage. Somewhere there's a photograph of us eating
at an In-N-Out Burger. I look fat. Another night we ate at Spago in the Forum.
Throughout the meal, I kept excusing myself and walking the streets of ancient Rome,
sky changing from day to night above me, to a phone booth in Caesar's Palace,
where I called to increase my bid on a NRFB Cinderella being auctioned in New Jersey.
I won it for $1,200.00. My need to possess what I wished I could have possessed that
Christmas morning in 1964, justifiable at the time, seems desperately sad to me now.

Also on my mantel, in a Plexiglas display case: my collection of vintage Yardley makeup: pink-
white-and-orange-striped Slicker tubes (fifteen of them), Glimmerick (*shimmers eyes*
like a thousand candles), frosted Sigh Shadow ("whisper-soft" brush-on eye powder
in such shades as Sealace and Rainbow Pink), Slicker nail polish, face Slicker, Oh! de London

cologne, London Lashes, Pot O' Gloss. I've even obtained, thanks to eBay, a
    Slicker whistle
and a Slicker key ring. Did you know that in 1968 Yardley of London
    "published"
their Poetry Collection, "six lyric, lacy lipsticks," "six love poems for lips":
    Couplet Coral,
Ballad Beige, Mauve Ode, Poetic Pink, Roundelay Rose, Sonnet Peach? Or
    that in 1971
they put out Slicker Lip Licks, so teenage girls could kiss "him" in his favorite
    flavor:
Raspberry, Strawberry, Rock Candy, Root Beer, Maple Sugar, Bubble Gum,
    Mint, Banana
Split? How many times must I return to the Thrifty Drug Store of my youth
    and
relive that initial, painful attachment? Just inside the automatic door, left
    through the
turnstile: the makeup counter. I can still see the woman behind it: her powder
    blue
Thrifty's smock, her glasses hanging by a chain around her neck, her perfect
    hair-sprayed
helmet of gray hair. The trick was to walk as slowly and nonchalantly as
    possible, taking in as
much of the Yardley display as I could in just a few seconds. I've written about
    this elsewhere:
"the rows of striped lipstick tubes pure eye candy." What must she have
    thought of this
obsessed trespasser in Cosmetics. He'd turn right, then two aisles over, left, to
    Toys.
More torture: the Barbie outfits in their pink-and-white-striped cardboard
    frames.
He'd pretend to be interested in the little bottles of model airplane paint. But
    he'd
be eyeing those chiffon and taffeta gowns, those high heels and necklaces and
    gloves
stitched into Mattel's colorful display packages. If he could pick up one of
    those
packages and press the dress, the accessories—the cellophane would make a
    crinkly sound.
He didn't know that housewives all over Japan, commissioned to work at home,

had strained their eyesight, pricked their fingers with needles, and hunched
    over
and wrecked their backs affixing Barbie's clothing to those captivating displays.
    Nor did he know
that three decades later he'd begin to collect the lipsticks and doll outfits he
    coveted from a distance.
NRFB: never removed, never handled by anyone since that Japanese housewife
    gently pulled
the white thread through the hem of the dress and, on the back of the card, tied
    a tight knot.

Also on my mantel, in a stack of books: Dodie Bellamy's latest, *Pink Steam.*
    Last year,
after a visit to Chicago, she wrote: "I keep thinking about your Yardley vitrine."
In the eighties, in San Francisco to do a reading, Kevin and Dodie drove me to
the Barbie Hall of Fame in Palo Alto. Somewhere there's a photo (Kevin took
    it)
of me standing in front of a case of Barbies. My destiny—though I couldn't
    have foreseen
it then. It wasn't until 1993 or 4, rummaging through a cardboard box at the
    23rd St.
flea market, that I would discover Francie's phonograph and garter belt.
    Francie,
Barbie's teenaged "MOD"ern cousin, was created in 1966, Mattel's attempt to
    reflect
the swinging youth culture. Shorter and less busty than Barbie, Francie came
    with "real"
eyelashes and an infinitesimal mascara brush. The phonograph was part of
    Dance Party,
an outfit that included pink crepe dress, white hose, pink heels, two records
    (one
with a blue label, one a red; both said "Barbie"), chocolate sundae, spoon, and
    napkin.
The garter belt (which had four pink plastic garters) came with First Things
    First,
a lingerie set—white nylon sprinkled with brightly colored flowers—"to go with
all of Francie's fab outfits!" Which I watched my sisters unwrap, uninterested
    in my Christmas

presents. That morning, Ira had dragged me to the flea market. And there I
    stood, in the
middle of Chelsea, holding Francie's diminutive garter belt in the palm of my
    hand. So
my collecting began, and I went far on my own pink steam. Somewhere there
    are photos
of the display cases in Ira's and my loft. Lynn Crosbie wrote about them in
    Phoebe 2002:

> "Don't touch anything in the display cases!" David said,
> and I stared at them for hours.
>
> The tableaus of Barbies, Midges, and Skippers,
> reclining, posing, babysitting, and so on,
>
> each dressed to the nines.
>
> The kitchen was fully detailed, and included
> plates, silverware, a turkey roasting in an oven.

The best moment was when M.G. Lord, author of *Forever Barbie*, came to
    dinner.
She studied the dolls (over a hundred at that point) then said, "It takes a
    collector
to do it right." The worst was when Jeffery walked in and said, "Oh, how
    girlish."
Another low was when the lips on a blonde bubblecut disappeared before my
    eyes (exposure
to sunlight). I contacted a restorer well known in the Barbie collecting world.
We became friendly over the phone. I told her I wrote poetry; she expressed
    interest
in reading my work. I included a copy of *Answer.Song* when I mailed her the
    doll—
$8.00 for a repaint. When next we spoke, she was considerably less friendly.
    She'd
opened the book to "My Lover," an explicit litany of my sexual experiences;
was certain I'd intended to shock her. "You should be more careful who you
    show
this to. I loved Sylvester when I was into disco, but this was too much for me."

———

Just three more pink threads and this poem will be finished. Poem I'm going to
    miss.
Poem which promised so much: *We know how to give our whole life every day.*
    Poem
which became, some time ago, as much about what I can't fit in as can. All
    those memories
crowding around the edges. How I once came out of a blackout on the San
    Diego Freeway,
doing 70. I'd been to a party at Dennis Cooper's. Was that the party he poured
    a drink on my head?
How that infuriated me. The same party I kissed Amy in the kitchen; she
    looked so sexy
in her red dress. Years later, when we talked about it, she said kissing me was
    like kissing
Virginia Woolf. Or how, in elementary school, I did a diorama of the Green
    Room
based on a photograph (in a spread on the White House) in *National
    Geographic.* What magic
I worked with a little cardboard, construction paper, and glue. I guess that's as
    close
as I could come to having my own dollhouse. I seem to recall that my teacher
    thought I
had cheated (help from parents), my diorama was that good. Or how Jeannie
    and I first met:
in either 1992 or 1993, on either the 13th or the 30th floor of the Empire State
    Building,
at a meeting of the NYBC (New York Barbie Club). *How does anything know
    its kind?*
Fate sat us next to each other; we discovered we knew each other's poems.
    What a gift
her friendship has been: to be able to share the ups and downs of two worlds:
    poetry
and collecting. How to make this all fit? Simply bounce here and there, like a
    time machine
gone haywire? Here I am in San Francisco, 1976, wearing my Emily Dickinson
    T-shirt.
Taped to the wall behind me: pictures of E.D. and Rimbaud (torn from library
    books)

and Anne Sexton's poem "Her Kind," which I'd written with magic marker on a sheet
of butcher paper. Here I am in London, sometime in the nineties, standing in front of
23 Fitzroy Road, the address where Sylvia Plath died. I wear an orange shirt and black blazer,
and dark sunglasses, so no one can see the eyes of this death monger, this gauche American.
Here I am back in Los Angeles, circa 1983: Elaine Equi and I wander through Hollywood
Memorial Cemetery in search of Rudolph Valentino's grave. The ghost of Clifton Webb
keeps us company. And here I am in Chicago, month before last, crying my eyes out over an
aborted affair. Don't worry, I won't put your name in my poem, pal, but you know who
you are: you of the mixed messages, you of the chickenshit emails, you of the disappear.
And the fear, the fear, the fear (as Anne, badly imitating Sylvia, would say). "Remember
that not getting what you want is sometimes a wonderful stroke of luck." Thank you,
Dalai Lama, for your quotable wisdom. And remember that unfortunate moment in bed:
"You make me want to fuck you." "I don't get fucked." Did that ever stop me in
my tracks. "Really?" Headshake: No. "Even over time, with intimacy and trust?"
Same headshake. If I had it to do over again, I'd say "Then why did you sit on me
and press my cock against your crack?" Ironic: I was always the one who didn't want
to get fucked: "I had a bad experience when I was young." Strange to be on the other
side of that Looking-Glass. What's the point of all that intense foreplay if it doesn't lead
to *acute core-reaching fucking?* Deep breath. Let him go. Bless you and fuck you.
Is that the best you can do? So much for acceptance. *I want a complete and equal love.*

A few loose ends (of the pink variety). This week Jeannie sends me a color xerox of an ad

from the June 1954 issue of *McCall's* magazine: "The Pink Shoe." Four scintillating styles.

In fine print beneath number two (*Wonderful with summer's whirling skirts is this delicate*

kid-stripping sandal): "Drawings by Andy Warhol." Chuck Stebelton sends me an email

announcing his new book, *Circulation Flowers*: "it's alarmingly pink!" "I'm enjoying

your pink correspondence with Elaine," Connie Deanovich wrote me in the mid-nineties,

after she read, in separate magazines, pink poems we'd dedicated to each other.

At the end of my drinking (early eighties), I often spoke on the phone with Michael Silverblatt.

In those small hours, Michael would recount his conversations with Pauline Kael.

One night he told me Kael was working on a review of *Sophie's Choice*, which I hadn't seen,

and described a scene in the movie where everything was pink. I said that reminded me

of the pink sequence in *What a Way to Go!* Then related the entire plot of that childhood favorite.

Sure enough, my association made its way into Kael's *New Yorker* review: "Was it

inspired by the 1963 movie *What a Way to Go!*, with Shirley MacLaine trying to

cheer up her husband, Pinky, by having the rooms in their mansion all painted pink?"

Kael gets several things wrong: the film came out in 1964, and it's Pinky (Gene

Kelly), not MacLaine, who out of sheer egotism douses their world with pink paint.

Obviously some fact checker couldn't have cared less about such pink minutiae. Michael

arranged for me to meet Pauline when I went to New York in October of '82. I visited her

in her *New Yorker* office. She was kind, given I was barely able to speak (awestruck),

and signed a copy of *Reeling* for me. I later gave that book away. And dropped
   Michael.
He'd have to wait ten years to get his revenge. When *Answer Song* came out,
   he
interviewed me for his radio show. He asked me to read a piece, then hit me
   with:
"What makes you think that is a poem?" It threw me; I shut tight as a clam.
   Thank God
that interview was unairable. If I had it to do over . . . Well, he was a low
   bottom friend.
At least Sheree, when she forbade me to participate in any of Bob's memorials,
   was aboveboard
about her anger. And Bob's: he never stopped railing at me, according to his
   Pain Journal,
even though I'd tried, a year before his death, to make things right. I'm grateful
   that
Henry and I were able to patch things up. Jeffery and I visited him when I was
   in New York
last April, two months before he died. It was hard to believe that nearly a
   decade and a half
had passed since the three of us last sat in Henry's kitchen and laughed. I
   thought it
serendipitous, since I was writing this when he died, that a memorial for Henry
should be held at a cafe called Pink Pony. Kept that pink coincidence in the
   back of my
mind. God bless Henry Flesh, who died ten pages shy of finishing his third
   novel.
And God bless Ed Smith, another old friend who died during the writing of this
   poem.
Ed who initially rubbed me the wrong way (I took his irreverence personally),
   but who,
once I got sober, I grew to appreciate. At news of his suicide, I reached for his
   books, and out fell,
from one of them, a slip of paper: this collaboration, signed by both of us,
   written on 10/30/88:

half
beautiful

                        don't
                        sway

                        point
                        north

You drive in a circle. A pink one. The first time I saw Barbie: Linda Moran
    invited me into
her backyard (I was seven or eight): there on a picnic table was a black patent
    leather
wardrobe case. She pulled back the clasp: inside, the blonde ponytail with big
    breasts,
but what really interested me were all the clothes hanging on little plastic
    hangers—
a white nurse's uniform, a tight-fitting black nightclub dress, a see-through pink
    negligee.
And the miniatures Linda poured out of the accessory drawers—a wooden bowl
    with three
balls of yarn and knitting needles, gloves and purses, tiny plastic high heels, a
    wax apple,
a pink stuffed dog—were bliss to behold. I remember that Linda's mother,
    Priscilla,
stood watching us from their living room window. (Fast forward to the nineties:
in a bus on the way to a doll show in Hackensack, New Jersey, I meet Cyndi,
    also on her way
to the show, who tells me that her mother was so into Barbie she used to wake
    her in the
middle of the night and ask, "What happened to Barbie's sunglasses? Where's
    Barbie's comb?")
My first memory: January 31, 1957 (I was three and a half), 11:18 a.m.,
    Pacoima, California:
two airplanes collide in the clear skies over the San Fernando Valley: one of
    them,
its left wing sheared off, begins a steepening, high velocity dive earthward and
    slams
into a Pacoima churchyard, killing all four crew members on board. Upon
    impact,
hundreds of pieces of flaming metal and debris slash across the playground of
    Pacoima

Junior High School, where some 220 boys are just ending their outdoor athletic
    activities.
Several boys are killed. I remember that our house shook, that I was watching
    cartoons
on TV. My mother was vacuuming in another room. I also remember my
    mother,
hysterical, dragging me across a vacant lot; my brother was in the elementary
    school
across the street from the junior high. *Your destination waits where you left it:*
    Thrifty Drug
in Chatsworth, week of July 5, 1967 (I was almost fourteen): I spin the paper-
    back rack
like the wheel of fortune: it stops at a novel with "dolls" in the title, its white
    cover
spattered with red, blue, and green-and-yellow pills. My life will never be the
    same.
"Pink will always be there for you," Elaine said the other day, when I said I was
    sad the poem
was coming to an end. "I've never forgotten how deep and important our
    friendship was,"
Eileen said in an email a year ago. Did she know how meaningful that would
    be for me?
When I was dealing with a disgruntled colleague, Laura Mullen said, "Yes, but
    you're a
whole person, David." One of the nicest things anyone's ever said to me. I'm
    grateful
that on her deathbed my mother said: "You've been a good son." And that
    when Allen Ginsberg
died, tulips Ira and I had sent were in the room. Were they red? Pink? *You*
    drive in a circle.
I can still hear Allen say, after reading one of my poems in a workshop at
    Brooklyn College,
"Where's the epiphany, Trinidad?" Somewhere there's a photograph of us
    standing
in front of St. Mark's Church. I wear a red shirt. Recently, I came across some
notes I'd taken, many years ago, during a session with a psychic. I'd asked her
    about rape:

vital attention from
powerful person –
that's why it's exciting

Still, in my red journal, a few months before starting this poem, I asked the
    question again.
You drive in a circle. (Both Maureen and Susan called in the last few minutes.
    "I can't talk,
I'm at the end of my long poem." Thank God for my friends.) In 1993, I asked
    Amy
to sign *Nerve Storm*. She wrote: "For David, A Doll who needs no valley". In
    1982,
I asked Lewis MacAdams to sign *Africa and the Marriage of Walt Whitman and*
    Marilyn Monroe.
He said: "What should I write?" "Bliss in this life," I said, quoting one of his
    poems.
He smiled and jotted it down. At the end of fourth grade, I asked a substitute
    teacher
to sign my blue autograph book. I regret that in the late eighties, in a fit of
    purge,
I threw that book away; I wish I could include her name. But I've never
    forgotten
what she wrote: "David, you are an unusual boy. May it continue into adult
    life."

July 22, 2004 – December 16, 2005

Notes

KID STUFF BY OSCAR WILDE

"Wham-O created the Water Wiggle, a wacky-looking plastic head that attached to the end of any hose and turned it into a wild, water-spraying snake that propelled itself willy-nilly as kids ran screaming for cover." From *The Toy Book* by Gil Asakawa and Leland Rucker.

CLASSIC LAYER CAKES

This piece was inspired by Kimiko Hahn's "Sewing without Mother."

Most reincarnational philosophies teach . . . From *Reincarnation: A New Horizon in Science, Religion, and Society* by Sylvia Cranston and Corey Williams.

I wish I could do this memory better. Patricia Spears Jones.

A POEM UNDER THE INFLUENCE

Of such moments is happiness made. Anne Sexton.

Holly was not a girl who could keep anything . . . Truman Capote.

Pocketa-pocketa. Anne Sexton.

Lawsamercy, honeychil'! What you spect? 'Taint like you was . . . See Truman Capote's "Nocturnal Turnings" in *Music for Chameleons*.

We know how to give our whole life every day. Arthur Rimbaud, translated by Louise Varèse.

How does anything know its kind? Jeanne Marie Beaumont.

acute core-reaching fucking. Anaïs Nin.

I want a complete and equal love. Anaïs Nin.

You drive in a circle. Ted Hughes.

Your destination waits where you left it. Ted Hughes.

Photo: Nick Carbó

David Trinidad's books include *Phoebe 2002: An Essay in Verse* and *Plasticville*, both published by Turtle Point Press. With Denise Duhamel and Maureen Seaton, he edited *Saints of Hysteria: A Half-Century of Collaborative American Poetry* (Soft Skull Press, 2007). He currently teaches poetry at Columbia College Chicago, where he co-edits the journal *Court Green*.